Primary Education

DPH Education Series

PRIMARY EDUCATION

By

U.K. Singh
&
K.N. Sudarshan

DISCOVERY PUBLISHING HOUSE PVT. LTD.
NEW DELHI-110 002

First Published-1996
Reprinted-2011

ISBN 81-7141-357-9

Published by
DISCOVERY PUBLISHING HOUSE PVT. LTD.
4383/4A, Ansari Road, Darya Ganj
New Delhi-110 002 (India)
Phone: +91-11-23279245, 43596064-65
Fax: +91-11-23253475
E-mail: parul.wasan@gmail.com
discoverypublishinghouse@gmail.com
web: www.discoverypublishinggroup.com

Printed at:
Dynamic Printers
Delhi

Preface

The *DPH Education Handbook* has been created to provide access to information about contemporary topics in education. Practitioners and students at all levels in education have a need to know what is happening today, in addition to historical treatments within the literature.

Each chapter within the Handbook is designed to provide the user with needed "state-of-the-art" information as well as further sources of information. One of the significant features of each chapter is the inclusion of specific programmes, projects and activities so that the researcher can locate human resources as well as the literature.

The handbook will be of use to graduate and post graduate students in education and to practicing teachers, administrators, librarians and planners. The chapters and the further sources of information cited in each book should lead the reader to thousands of people and documents for either research or programme planning purposes.

An effort to achieve universal and effective education is based on a recognition of the rights of students to basic education that enables them to thrive in a complex society, as well as a realization the technological and economic growth is facilitated by increasing the numbers of students, even those with poor academic progresses, who are, in fact successful in learning. Thus, recent and current efforts improve education serve both private and social interests.

This series is addressed to administrators, planners and educators working in the field of education and training with a view to stimulating interest and attention in the areas of education and its related fields. It is also addressed to a growing number of teachers and instructors who will be practitioners in education and who will need to be acquainted with the modern aspects of educational practice and development. Many ideas, generalisations and discussions presented in this series should also prove useful to employing organisations committed to provide training facilities within their establishments—leading to effective mutual participation by institutions and organisations.

The editors wishes to thank the contributors, as well as those organizations that gave permission to publish their extracts, chapters etc.

Editors

Contents

1 The Development of Primary Education

Origins of infant and nursery schools

The work of Robert Owen, of Froebel, the development of Froebelianism, and the original thought of Maria Montessori will be discussed in later chapters. Their general influence upon the methods in both nursery and infant schools has been clearly marked in the history of those departments since the turn of the century. The Forster Act of 1870 emphasized the value and significance of separate infant schools or of infant classes in elementary schools, and infant education was firmly brought into the elementary system with the age of give fixed as the age of admission.

Whilst there was some general acceptance for the need of nursery and infant education, there were those educationists who also saw the desperate need for changes in the environmental conditions of young children. In particular, the sisters Rachel and Margaret McMillan engaged in a campaign not merely to establish nursery schools but also to make adequate provision for the physical care and development of young children. In 1907 the Board of Education has referred the age of admission of young children to school to the Consultative Committee, and their Report in 1908 discussed the general work and influence of nursery schools, expressing the opinion that the age of three should not be regarded as too young for those children for whom such schools were considered necessary. Mean while the McMillan sisters were not merely pressing for the provision of school means, regular medical inspections and health centres for poor children, they were acting upon their convictions. In 1908 they opened their first schools clinic at Bow, and in 1911 they developed the first real nursery school at Deptford.

Their concept of a nursery school was in reality a large space of ground where the children could live in the open air and enjoy natural activity and play. It was a garden, a kindergarten, with shelters where the children could go when the weather was inclement and where they could continue their activities without interruption. The sisters believed that the children, both rich and poor, should come under the influence of this environment for a long as possible; and so their school day, which seem perhaps to us rather lengthy, began at 8.00 a.m. and went on 5.00 or 6.30 p.m. But this was not a day of formal tuition or instruction; it was a day of natural interest and activity, with two and sometimes three meals provided, and an enforced period of rest after lunch. The McMillan had in mind that if you wanted to formulate the character and personality of the child you had to provide the right sort of environment for it during the most impressionable years of its life, and for as long as possible during its active day.

Rachel McMillan died in 1917 but Margaret continued the work until her own death in 1931. In 1918 the local education authorities were employed to make arrangements for supplying or helping the supply of nursery schools and classes for children over two and under five years of age, where such schools and classes were considered to be essential for the healthy physical and mental development of the children concerned. Thus the State, through local authorities, gradually took on the responsibility for the early years of the child's development. And the schools that it began to produce at least had the experimental experience of the efforts of the McMillans, who had emphasized throughout the importance of free movement in play, of the feelings and emotions in personal development, and of the Froebelian principle of education through imagination. Many of the local nursery schools, of course, did not have the basic 'space area' as conceived by the McMillans, nor the gardens, shrubs, lawns and green-housed. But the Froebelian and Montessorian principles made their impact; they view that the only real form of education is self-education was well entrenched in nursery and infant educational developments.

By 1938 there were 46 nursery schools maintained by L.E.A.s and 57 by voluntary management; in 46 the number had dropped to a total of 92. It must be remembered; however, that during the ear years a very large number of day nurseries and nursery schools had been established by the welfare authorities, and at the end of the war these were handed over to the L.E.A..s. In consequence, in 1947 the total number of nursery schools had risen to 370,17 of which were now provided by voluntary institutions. in january 1965 the total number of nursery schools under the supervision of the Department of Education and Science reached 639, and the number of pupils in these schools was 27,909. Of these schools 436 were maintained on direct grant.

Whether or not 'Heaven lies about us in our infancy', as Wordsworth insisted, the importance of both nursery and infant education cannot be over-estimated. on the infant schools in Britain, Martin Mayer has said that they are 'probably the world's most ambitious pattern of beginning instruction'. But there is still a great neglect in our society of nursery education; the total number of children actually in nursery schools in January 1965 represented only about 7 per cent of the total number of children in the age groups 0-4, i.e., 4,100,000. And when all the children under five in all institutions under the supervision of the Ministry of health, the Home Office and the L.E.A.s were taken into account, the total number was still only 283,000, i.e. 6.9 per cent of the total number of children under five years of age. The Central Advisory Council for Education recommended in its Report in 19678 that there should be a large expansion of nursery education, and that such education should be available to children at any time after the beginning of the schools year after they reach the age of three until they reach the age of compulsory schooling. over the country as a whole it was considered that provision should be made for 15 per cent of children to attend both a morning and afternoon session.

The advisory Council felt that full-time nursery education for children whose mothers could not satisfy the authorities that they has exceptionally good reasons for working should be given a low priority. It was also recommended that the education of children over three in day nurseries should be the responsibility of the education department rather than of the health department. It went on to say that

'Ideally, all services, including nursery, for the care of young children should be grouped together and placed near the children's homes and the primary schools. The planning of new areas and the rebuilding of old should take account of nursery education'.

Legislation : 1870-1918

We have already mentioned that the Education Act of 1870 did not really introduced free, compulsory elementary education for all, but compulsion was placed upon school boards to provide schools where necessary; the Elementary Education a Act of 1876 was the first Act to put compulsion upon parents in order to ensure that their children received education which was efficient at least in reading, writing and arithmetic. The movement was towards free education, for even the 1870 Act restricted fees to 9d per week and gave powers to school boards to pay fees for poorer children.

In 1888 the Cross Commission made it clear that the idea of separate junior Departments was becoming increasingly more explicit. This was due in the main to the growth of Higher Grade Schools. From the time of the Cross Report to the end of the century many schools boards were grading their elementary schools into junior, Middle and Senior Departments. This is interesting in view of the more recent nonmenclature of First, Middle and Third Schools.

The Balfour-Morant Education Act of 1902 abolished the school boards and created in their place the local education authorities. The major L.E.A.s were councils of the counties and county boroughs, whilst the minor L.E.As were boroughs with a population of more than 10,000, and urban districts of more than 20,000. These minor L.E.A.s possessed powers over elementary education only. All L.E.A.s were given the duties and powers of the former school boards and attendance committees, and they were obliged to maintain and keep efficient all public elementary schools, whether council or voluntary, and to control all secular education in voluntary elementary schools in the area.

In 1904 a new elementary code was produced which incorporated the changes proposed by the

Balfour-Morant Act. The code has what Professor E.J. R. Eaglesham calls' a cleverly written preface' which he further claims was a statement of 'training in followership rather than leadership training', and suited more to the working classes than to the middle and upper classes. No one would deny that whoever wrote the preface- Sir Robert Morant or professor J.M. Mackail- it was cleverly composed. Indeed, a detailed examination of its content makes one wonder whether Eaglesham's stigmatization of 'training in followership' is justifiable. After Lowe's revised code of 1862, and its payment by results, one is naturally impressed by the somewhat more philosophical and educational tone of the introduction to the 1904 code. But Morant was clearly not concerned to develop elementary education by the provision of more resources: in face Eaglesham suggests that there is evidence to support the conclusion, however cynical, that *'Morant aimed at and achieved a standstill in elementary education'.*

But cynicism should not lead us to derogate from the essential educational values made explicit in th e introduction to the code, which may well of course have been a philosophical sop to compensate for a lack of practical assistance. But it was a an organized attempt to state in straightforward ad simple terms the purpose of the public elementary school; this was 'to form and strengthen the character and to develop the intelligence of the children entrusted to it, and to make the best use of the school years available, in assisting both girls and boys according to their different needs, to fit themselves, practically as well as intellectually, for the work of life'.

There is here a recognition of the child as a total being who has specific and differing needs within the realms of character and intellect, and additionally the need to be initiated into the world of work and life itself in such a way as to be able to cope practically as well as intellectually. Eaglesham may be right when he comments that whilst there is to be preparation for life there is to be no vocational education. But it is a stage further than the three Rs. The children are to be trained in habits of careful observation and clear reasoning so that they may gain san intelligent acquaintance with some of the facts and laws of nature' and this is hardly 1followership'! The school must further arouse in its pupils a lively interest in man's ideals, achievements, literature and history; it must give them 'some power over language as an instrument of thought and expression'—surely more keeping with education for leadership! All sound education should make pupils and students aware of the limitations of their knowledge and encourage a due sense of humility within the realms of learning-whether they are leaders of followers. The code consequently adds that, while the school should make pupils conscious of their limitations it should, thoughtful study as will enable them to increase that knowledge' when their school career is over, and by their own efforts. This, indeed, is still one of the prime purpose of education-to demonstrate to pupils how to acquire knowledge and learning for themselves.

The influence in practice of the 'sloyd' movement is to be seen in other elements of the introduction which suggests that the school should encourage the natural activities of th child's hand and eye 'by suitable forms of practical work and manual instruction'; and the general, though gradual, movement towards hygiene and health is suggested by the training of pupils in physical exercises, organized games and the simple laws of health.

It is true that the code saw the possibility of discovering 'individual children who show promise of exceptional capacity', and that such children should be qualified to pass at the appropriate age into the secondary schools and there be enabled to derive the maximum benefit from the education offered them. Whilst this was a recognition that some children rather that others were fitted for further education it is worthy of note that there was a clause in parenthesis which had in mind the sort of contention which many educators have put forward in more recent years against the streaming of children in primary schools for the 11 + examination, and the gearing of the whole of the primary curriculum for the benefit of the academic few- 'to develop their special gifts.

The introduction was not an exhortation to industry, respect and reverence in quire the same sense as that implied in pervious codes and reports. There was little or no suggestion of 'followship' subservience in the terminology of th code. It was implied that there was a great responsibility on the part of the teachers to lay the foundations of conduct; and by their influence, example and personal sense of discipline, which should pervade the school, to inclucate in the children 'habits of industry, self control, and courageous perserance in the face od difficulties'- training suited, surely, to the middle and upper classed as well as the working classes. Reverence was to be taught, not for the nobility bur for what was noble; and children were to be ready for self-sacrifice and to strive to the uttermost for purity and truth. The respect which was to be fostered was not that for 'their betters', but for others, 'which must be the foundation of unselfishness and the true basis of all good manner's. The corporate life of the school was the basis for the development of the instinct for fair play and sense of loyalty to one another-the very 'germ of a wider sense of honor in later life'. Indeed some of the introduction, for good or ill, reads almost like a public school code.

The introduction concludes that school, parents and home should all unite in an effort to enable the children to reach their fullest development a individuals, and also to become useful and upright citizens in their community. Whether Morant was interested in forwarding elementary education or not, there was a certain liberalizing and humanizing purpose expressed in this introduction. And this was supported by the Blue Book issued by the Board of Education in

1905, which was a handbook of suggestions for teachers involved in the work of public elementary schools. The Blue Book suggested that uniformity of practice throughout such schools was not desirable, but rather that each teacher should think for himself and work out his own methods according to the school's conditions and requirements. Above all the teacher should know and sympathize with the children he was teaching. The entire process of education was viewed as a 'partnership for the acquisition of knowledge'. Facts were not to be dealt with in isolation but in relation to the total experience of the child- 'each lesson must be a renewal and an increase of that connected store of experience which becomes knowledge'

The Blue Book was in line with the introduction to the code in that it insisted that the latter should fully realize his duty to use his innate powers to the best advantage. Life must be presented as something at once pleasant ad serious, and in consequence the work being pursued in the schools was in a real sense a preparation for life. Moreover, the teacher's influence in all this was a very vital one, however short tha period of influence might be.

The First Education Act of 1918 enforced compulsory attendance at school up to the age of fourteen years, and it also underlined the need for a complete re-organization of what today is more specifically referred to as primary education, that is, the education of young children below the age of eleven years. All fees were completely abolished in public elementary schools, and all L.E.A.s were required to provide 'practical instruction suitable to the ages, abilities and requirements of the children; The L.E.A.s were also empowered to supply, or help supply, nursery schools for children over two years of age and under five, ' whose attenance at such schools is necessary for their healthy physical and mental development'. When he introduced the Education Bill, as President of the Board of Education, on August 10, 1917, Mr. H.A.L. Fisher concluded by suggesting that the rising generation could be protected against the deleterious effects of industrial pressures only by a further measure of State compulsion. But, he argued, the compulsion proposed in this Bill will be 'no sterilizing restriction of wholesome liberty, but an essential condition of a larger and more enlightened freedom, which will tend to stimulate the civic spirit, to promote general culture and technical knowledge, and to diffuse a steadier judgment and a better-informed opinion through the whole body of the community'.

The Hadow reports and after

In 1925 the Board of Education published *Circular 1350* which pointed out that the age of eleven was increasingly recognized as the 'most suitable dividing line between what may be called "Junior" and "Senior" education'. In 1926 the Hadow Report on *The Education of the Adolescent* clearly stated in Section 99 that.

'It is desirable that education up to 11 +

should be known by the general name of Primary Education, and after 11 by the general name of Secondary Education...'

Thus, the concept of 'primary education ' as a distinct area of development was fully established five years before the next report the next report of the Consultative Committee appeared. Certainly the Board did everything it could to keep the concept alive, and after its publication in 1928. *The new Prospect in Education*, L.E.A.s drew up schemes for the full provision of 'post primary' education for children of 11 + along th lines indicated in the Hasow Report.

There can be little doubt that the later Hasow Report of 1931, *The Primary School*, was one of the most important that the Consultative Committee produced. There is a tendency to look upon it as little more than a historical curiosity; certainly beside the Plowden Report of 1967 it appears a very slim and modest volume, indeed, and although it took two years to produce its gross cost was minute compared with the cost of Plowden. After a fairly lengthy introduction on general principles, the report provided a historical sketch of the development of the idea of primary education from the beginning of the nineteenth century. It went on to describe the physical and mental development of children between the ages of seven and eleven; and it is interesting to note that, just as Plowden leans quite heavily upon Piagetian thought, the 1931 report used and quoted Piaget's *Le Language et la Pensee chez l'Enfant,* published in France in 1923 and translated into english in 1926. Appendix II to the report by professor Cyril Burt, then psychologist to the London Country Council, referred to 'Piaget's brilliant studies'. Thus the members of the Consultative Committee were certainly abreast of the psychological developments of their time.

The report then went on to consider the age limits for the upper stage of elementary education, which it felt should be fixed at the age of eleven; that is, the transfer from the primary to the secondary school should take place between the ages of eleven and twelve. It went on to discuss in some detail the arguments against separate 'infant' and 'junior' schools, but finally recommended that, in those areas where it was possible, there should be separate schools for children below the age of seven, and that in all primary schools there ought to be a well-defined line of education between the younger and older children. The report made it pellucidly clear that the primary school should not be regarded merely as a `preparatory department for the subsequent stage': primary school course were to be planned and conditioned by the specific needs of the child at that particular phase in his development, both physical and mental. Its attitude towards promotion to the secondary stage was made quite an examination at the age of eleven', were not to control primary schools curricula or activity.

The internal organization of primary schools was next discussed, including such problems as the size of classes and co-education at the upper stage od primary education. The report adduced evidence from a variety of sources to establish that classes in junior schools should be kept small, preferably about thirty five, and it further made the point that it would be impossible to put into operation many of its suggestions if large classes were retained in primary schools. The size of primary classes was indeed on of the most urgent problems facing education administrators. Concerning co-education the conclusion was that there was no valid objection on general or sociological grounds, provided due regard was paid to the differing needs of girls and boys in games and physical activities generally. Problems of mental and educational retardation were considered in detail, and the chief causes, detection, diagnosis and treatment dealt with. Retarded children required special attention between the ages of seven and eleven, and it was recommended that special classes should be organized for this purpose and that they should be small.

The traditional curriculum of the public elementary school was next analyzed , and the general principles on which the upper stages of primary education should be based were elicited. The report considered the complexity of 1modern industrial civilization' and the bearing this has upon the work of the primary school. It emphasized the uselessness, as well as the innate danger, of seeking to inclucate what A.N. Whitehead has termed "inert ideas'; and it deplored and deprecated the fact that, whilst a great deal of teaching was good in the abstract, too little of it directly assisted children to enlarge and vivify their instinctive hold on the condition of life by 'enriching, illuminating and giving point to their growing experience. The report summed up its view of the curriculum and its purpose in the following words:

'The curriculum is to be thought of in terms of activity and experience rather than of knowledge to be acquired and facts to be stored. Its aim should be to develop in a child the fundamental human powers and to awaken him to the fundamental interests of civilized life so far as these powers and interests lie within the compass of childhood, to encourage him to attain gradually to that control and orderly management of his lectual discipline, to help his to discover the idea of duty and to ensure it, and to open out his imagination and his sympathies in such a way that he may be prepared to understand and to follow in later years the highest examples of excellence in life an conduct.'

In its further consideration of curriculum detail the report emphasized the desirability of devising new methods on approaching its various branches, and in particular dealt with the project method and 'centres of interest' as set against the traditional practice of treating the curriculum in terms of 'subjects'. It warned, however, against the dangers of such methods when used without due consideration or caution-music and drama were often merely '1dragged in' in order to fulfill what were regarded as the claims of a a principle.

The staffing of primary schools and the training of teachers were next considered, and it was argued that teachers with general qualification rather than specialists were best suited for work in primary schools. A brief survey was made of school premises, equipment, school and class libraries, visual and auditory aids to teaching, school visits and playing fields. There followed a discussion of examinations in primary schools and it was recommended that, in classifying pupils leaving the infant school, of consultation between the teachers concerned. Any classification should be merely provisional, and should be subject to frequent revision. The council felt that as the provision of various types of secondary education was extend in the way proposed in the report on *The Education of the Adolescent*, the need for selecting by competition those children who would pass on to grammar and selective modern schools would diminish. It was convinced, however, that some sort of qualifying test or examination would always be required for the purpose of calssifying pupils, and argued for the use of written papers in English an arithmetic as a basic test of capacity and attainment of children at the age of eleven, together with carefully devised group intelligence tests.

Throughout the report of *The Primary School* there was a lively sense of the needs of the children themselves. It considered that what any wise and good parent might desire for his own children was precisely what the nation as a whole must desire for all children. The primary school was on the way to becoming what it should be, namely, the common school of the whole population, 'so excellent and so genrally esteemed that all parents will desire their children to attend it.

in 1933 the Hadow Report on the *Infant and Nursery school* was published and, like its predecessor, it emphasized the need to build new schools for young children more on an open-air plan. It also made it clear that the best place for very young children was in the home; but if this were not possible there was a great deal to be derive from attending nursery schools. Officialdom had learned a lot form the less orthodox and more progressive movements already mentioned, but despite all this many of the school building were inadequate and unhygienci. And despite the general desire expressed to make the primary school curriculum free from the pressures of selective examinations at the upper end of the school, in practice their classes were geared largely to preparation for secondary school work at the subject level and to some sort of 'scholarship' examination at 11+.

The White paper on *Education Reconstruction* which appeared in 1943, suggested in particular that children of 11 + should not be classified on the basis of a competitive test, but rather upon the assessment of their aptitudes based largely upon school records and intelligence tests. It felt that competitive examinations at the age of eleven were wrong in principle, not only because of the strain to which children were subjects but also not because of the stain to which children were subjected but also because the future schooling and careers of children were largely decided at this one point in time. It argued that at an age when children's minds were nimble and receptive, when their imagination and curiosity were strong and fertile, they were subjected to a cramping and stultifying curriculum in which considerable emphasis was placed upon 'ways and means or creating the examiners. The White Paper also stated that there should be separate schools for infants and juniors; and, whilst attendance was not compulsory before the age of five, L.E.A.s must make adequate provision for either nursery schools or, where these were considered expedient, nursery classes in infant schools.

The Butler Education Act of 1944 gave the primary school statutory authority in this country, and it defined primary education in Section 8 as 'full time education suitable to th requirements of junior pupils', who in years. The Act forced a clear break between primary and post-primary education: between primary and secondary schools, We are not here secondary education, the developing tripartite system, put ever-increasing pressures upon primary schools to act as forcing-grounds for grammar schools. The aims, so clearly expressed in the Hadow Report on *The Primary*

School, were very soon forgotten in the cut-throat competition for grammar school places, and the more enlightened development of primary school methods was somewhat delayed. There was a very real sense in which the firm, separate, statutory establishment of primary and post-primary educational institutions postponed the liberation of primary school methods for some years; and the Central Advisory Council for Education was probably not being over-pessimistic when it stated in 1947 that the gap between a reasonable provision of primary schools and the existing provision was formidable" 'half a century's unremitting efforts will be required before we can hope to have good primary schools for all'. A lot, of course, depends on the connotation of the word 'good' in this context: the verdict of the Plowden Report, twenty years later, was quite simply expressed in th words, 'the primary schools are giving good value for the inadequate among of money spent on them'. But it made it quite clear tha the financial inadequancies has severe educational repercussions, as we shall presently see.

The Plowden Report 1967

In august 1963 the Central Advisory Council for Education was asked by Sir Edward Boyle, then Minister of Education, 'to consider primary education in all its aspects, and the transition to secondary education'. Their investigations began soon afterwards, in October 1963, under the chairmanship of Lady Plowden, and included among their council's members were Sir John Newsom, professor A.J. Ayer, Miss M. Brearly, Professor C.E. Gittins, and Brigadier L.L.Thwaytes. Their report was concluded in October 1966 when it was presented to Anthony Crosland, Secretary of State for Education and Science, and it was published in january 1967. Volume 1 presented the report, and Volume II the statistics derived from a national survey of 20,00 schools. The total cost of the report was slightly over 120,000.

Part one formed an introduction to the whole investigation and referred in particular to the close association between the home background and academic achievement. The importance to individual of his family and social background was emphasized, and among question raised in general terms was that of whether 'finding out' had really proved to be better than 'being told'.

The growth of the child, and stressed the enormously wide variability in physical and intellectual maturity amongst children of the same age, particularly during adolescence, and the tendency for children to mature physically earlier than formerly. It went on to discuss the interaction of heredity and environment, the stages of child development as outlined by Jean Piaget, and the measurement of I.Q. It found a correlation between children's I Q.s and parental occupations-the children of professional parents have an average I.Q. of 115, emphasized that the child was a total personality, and that its emotional, social and intellectual aspects were closely intertwined.

Some of the implications of this section include the fact that individual variations between children of the same age are so great that any class, however apparently homogeneous, must always be treated as a body of children needing individual and different attention. Until a child is ready to take a particular step forward, it is useless to try and teach him to take it. Since any child grows up intellectually, emotionally, and physically at different rates, his teachers need to know and take account of his'developmental age' in all three respects. The child's physique, personality and capacity to learn will develop as a result of continuous interaction between his genetic inheritance and his environment. Whilst the genetic factors are not as yet under our control, the environmental factors largely are, part Two of the report, therefore, suggested the need of a very personal approach to the pupil in the primary school, with a special study of each child's 'readiness' for any particular form of learning or operation; and, at the same time, the provision of a sound, healthy, amenable sort of environment in order to present the best learning situations and conditions.

A minimum programme was suggested for the participation of parents in the education of children-a welcome to the school, meetings with teachers, open days, information for parents via brochures about the organization of the school, and reports for parents. There should be a concerted that the primary school should be used as fully as possible, out of ordinary school hours, as a sort of community centre. Community schools should be developed in all areas, but particularly in educational priority areas, where there was need for constant communication between parents and teachers if the schools' aims were to be completely understood. The report emphasized the need for colleges of education to have stronger and more efficient links with such schools and to develop courses to meet the needs of immigrant children in particular.

There was a very strong suggestion that the training of teachers genrally should take more account of those social factors which affect school performance, and also of the structure and functions of the school services. It recommended the initiation of experimental schemes in the joint training of teachers and social workers, and already there are colleges of education which are devising courses for social and youth wing work as well as general welfare work. The report made it very clear indeed that the primary school has a social role in the community, as well as an immediate and individual adductive role.

Part Four examined structure of primary education and divided the 20,000 schools surveyed into nine different categories, ranging from Category One to Category Nine. the report insisted that there ought to be a large expansion of nursery education, and that a start should be made as soon as possible. It went on to suggest that the entry to the infant school should be gradual between the ages of three years and five years via part-time attendance; the existing transition from home to school was too abrupt. There should be *three* years in the infant school and children should not be transferred until the age of 8 years; this would permit both children and teachers to work steadily and without anxiety.

The age for admission to a secondary school was suggested as 12 +, since this would give a *four-year* course in the junior or middle school, with a median age range from 8 years 6 months to 12 years 6 months. It should be noted here that the definition of primary education provided by Section 8 of the 1944 Education Act was amended by Section 3 of the 1948 Education Act. Primary education was there defined as 'full time education for children below 10 years 6 moths and children above that age but below 12 years who it is expedient to educate with them'; whilst the 1964 Education Act allowed proposals to be submitted to the Secretary of State for the establishment of new schools with age limits below 10 years 6 months and above 12 years. the report emphasized the need for the fullest possible documentation of each pupil before transfer to the secondary school, and it detailed the type of contents that a folder on each child should contain. A chapter on ~selection for Secondary Education' suggested that the ill effects upon primary education of selection for secondary schools were lessening, and the council recommended that authorities still employing selection procedures should no longer rely on an externally imposed battery of attainment and intelligence tests.

Part five dealt with the children in the schools, with curriculum and internal organization. Among a large variety of aims and purposes mooted, and dangers to be avoided, the following aims of primary education were accepted in somewhat general terms, with the proviso that generalities have limited value and can quickly become little more than platitudes; it was agreed that 'a pragmatic approach to the purposes of education was more likely to be fruitful'.

(a) Adaptability-to fir children for the society into which they will grow up, and to train them to be capable of adjusting to their changing environment.

(b) The all-round development of the individual child.

(c) The acquisition of the basic skills necessary in contemporary society.

(d) The religious and moral development of the child.

(e) Physical health, intellectual development, emotional and moral health, aesthetic awareness, a valid perspective, practical and social skills, and personal fulfilment.

(f) Values and attitudes must be mediated to the children. The school is not merely a teaching shop but a living community in which pupils learn primarily to live as children and not as future adults.

The work of Piaget was emphasized as a sound developmental approach to children's learning, and the importance of children's 'cultural' play was made clear. The report went on to consider certain particular aspects of the curriculum, and throughout there was an enlightened approach to both content and method, and a balanced attitude towards heuristic principles. The council has no doubt that 'children's questions about sex ought to be answered plainly and truthfully whenever they are asked' . It gave validity to the modern, both relaxed and friendly, approach within the primary schools as a much better preparation for life in contemporary society than th old authoritative one. Whilst accepting 'discipline", the council were clear that this connoted neither heavy punishment nor soft and flabby relationships; discipline, it felt, was impaired by such elements as disorder, untidiness and slackness- it could flourish only in an ethos of order an purposefulness, in which boredom had been eliminated. There must be, in all this, a healthy combination of individual, group, and class work and learning. Due consideration was also given to the education of both handicapped and gifted children.

The role of the teacher was discussed, and it was argued that teachers must enlarge their endeavors and enlist to a greater extent parents' interest in their children's education. It was extremely important to diagnose the child's needs and potentialities and there would be increasing demands on the knowledge of the teacher, whether literary, scientific or mathematical. Teachers, said the Report, 'cannot escape the knowledge that children will catch values and attitudes far more from what teachers do than what they say. unless they are courteous, they cannot expect courtesy from children: when teaches are eager to learn and turn readily to observation and to books, their pupils are likely to do the same'

The report, in effect, asked not only for more teachers but also for better quality ones. It went on to discuss teachers' aides, or trained ancillaries, who might give substantial help to teachers inside and outside the classroom, and who would have equal status with nursery assistants and have comparable training. The council considered that colleges of education, in general, were too remote from the problems of the school; it recommended a full inquiry into the system of training of teachers, and suggested that there should be more joint appointments to college and school staffs. Further, a network of residential teachers' courses should be developed.

(i) The Department of Education and Science should consider taking steps which would require all independent schools to state on their prospectuses whether the schools were recognized or registered and what this implies. The Department of Education and Science should reconsider the terms "recognized" and "registered" and try to devise more informative ones.

(ii) The Secretary of State's powers to serve Notices of Complaint on independent schools should be based on more stringent criteria. The construction of ~objectionable" should be widened to include any conditions, physical or educational, in which children's welfare was not thought to be adequately safeguarded.

(iii) All head teachers of independent schools should be qualified teachers. After a data to be specified, only qualified teachers should be appointed as heads in new schools, or when there is a change of head teacher.

(iv) In-service courses should wherever possible allow some places for teachers from independent schools. The independent schools themselves should take through their professional organizations to "increase the facilities for in-service training for teachers in independent schools'

The primary schools were giving good value for the inadequate amount of money spent on them' , and went on th state that teachers were too few in number and too unevenly distributed to do the job adequately. The first priority was the establishment of education priority areas; the recruitment of teachers' aides would be an essential and immediate source of help to the schools everywhere, the essential improvement of bad primary school buildings must be undertaken as soon as possible wherever they existed; and nursery education must be extended through increased accommodation and staff. Planning should begin on changes in the national dates of entry, and also on the ages of transfer between the different stages of primary education.

The Plowden Report represents one of the most through investigations into any area of education over produced. Perhaps not least of its achievements was its virtual unanimity, which is reflection on the goodwill and singleness of purpose of its twenty-five members over a period of three years of intensive work and study. Out of every 100 women who enter our colleges of education, only 47 will be in the schools after three years of teaching; and after six years of service only 30 will remain. Perhaps the most sanguine way to look at the figures is simply to argue that 70 women out of every 100 so trained have, at least, qualified in a profession to which they may later return, but in any case they have found one way of obtaining higher education, with often minimum of entry qualifications; and as mothers, in the majority of cases, they will have a better understanding of educational problems. It is certainly not a bad thing for future mothers both to be well educated and to have a professional qualification in reserve.

2 The Teacher and the Purpose of Primary Education

There are some truth universally acknowledged but about which little is done. It is an ancient wisdom, not confined to the Jusuits, that the essential character of people, their attitudes and motivation, are formed in their early years. It is also a new wisdom, reiterated in many research studies, that the earliest experiences of childhood and their subsequent development give the basis both for ability and what the individual does about it. The only questions is whether the parents and other adults are the most important influence, or whether the initial experiences of schooling have an equally powerful effect. What is not in question is the understanding that the earlier years of education are more formative than the later ones.

And yet, no amount of evidence seems to make a difference to the way in which primary education, in the broadest sense, is regarded. Adults look back with self-conscious familiarity on their experiences at secondary school and in higher education, when they were more aware of what they were learning, and less aware of being taught. Over the gulf of the years lies an almost deliberate forgetfulness that makes the experience of primary schools seem like an alien territory. It is far easier to look back, with the hindsight of more recently acquired knowledge, than to grasp the developing thoughts of one's younger self exploring the environment with precision and panache. Our later point of view can be singular and egocentric; as if we become less and less aware of our dependence on the past.

One of the clearest sings of the general lack of understanding of the importance of primary schools is the misunderstanding of the role of teachers in them. It is a universal problem. In many countries elementary teachers undergo a completely separate system of training, both shorter and less rigorous than that of their secondary counterparts, as if it were less demanding to teach younger children. Their very expertise as teachers is not rated as highly as the ability to know a particular subject well. This distinction between recognition of the importance of good teaching and expertise in one part of the curriculum is shared by the children themselves. By the time they leave primary school, children believe that it is only a preparation for the important events to come; that secondary school is more significant and that all education leads to the pursuit of qualifications for jobs. The dominating difficulty in the purpose of primary schools is the fact that 'knowing' is rated more highly than 'teaching', despite the importance of the latter and its equally intimate connection with 'learning'.

The distinct role of the primary school, often seen in terms of conveying essential skills - reading and writing and arithmetic - as well as the ability to mix in the society of others, it itself being eroded. We note the growing recognition of the part that parents can play. The primary teacher is therefore no longer seen as the only expert on whom the parent must wait so that the child can be instructed. Nor is the school any longer seen as the place where all the deficiencies of home can be compensated. The recognition of the more subtle skills of learning, through relationships and through motivation, through the home and pre-school experiences, means that the singular purpose of primary schools is less easily defined.

The erosion of the traditional position of the primary school teacher also takes place at the point where children move on. There have been many experiments with middle schools, on the grounds that the transition from primary school to secondary school, from generalism to specialism, cannot be handled by the primary schools themselves. From the Primary Survey of 1978 onwards the government has been concerned to make the primary teacher more of a specialist, playing the role of consultant to colleagues as well as handling the complexities of a large class. The training of primary school teachers is not only marked by the growing number of those who enter the profession after a specialized first degree followed by a postgraduate certificate, but the demand that *all* should have at least two years of a 'subject study'. A simplified notion of the curriculum was first evident in the criteria laid down on teacher training, long before the national framework. On the one hand, the primary teacher is seen to be more dependent on, and answerable to, the parents and the community. On the other hand, the primary teacher is defined as a specialist, not as a specialist teacher, but as a specialist in a particular area of the curriculum.

One of the reasons for this conflict in attitudes derives from the very image that primary schools have tended to project, whether they liked it or not. For the 'general public' the virtues of primary schools have been associated with comfortable stability, where children's happiness has been deemed more important than their academic advance, as if the two were in opposition to each other. The desire to make children feel at home in strange circumstances, with other children, and to foster in them a sense of personal well-being, has given primary schools a particular ethos. The children themselves contrast their sense of the comfort of the primary school against that of the bustle and demands of the secondary. At best such a sense of security suggest that children's well-being is forested in a variety of ways, that they are free to explore ideas, to ask questions and fulfil their own talents. At worst, such emphasis on security can seem to outsiders as wasteful, not making enough demands and not matching appropriate tasks to the ability of children.

One of the abiding concerns in the educational system general is what Hargreaves calls the "cult of individualism'. At the primary schools this can be projected as 'child centred' in the sense of a belief in the autonomy of the individual child and his innate ability to be creative and imaginative. The problem with such a view of children's own capacities is that it leads to the assumption that schools can do little to compensate for the problems of society or the child's home background. If a child is an autonomous learner it can be argued that each has to find his own way of learning, at the same time as adapting to the many rules of behaviour, both explicit and implied, that the school presents. This can be difficult for children. If we observe children in a primary school, nothing their experiences rather than being caught up in the demands of our own teaching, it is clear that from the child's point of view some of the impressions of school are not part of the school's intentions.

It is impossible for schools to make everything explicit but there are many ambiguities for children. Despite the emphasis on achievement and concentration, children spend a significant proportion of the day waiting for things to happen. They are puzzled by the relationship between work and play. Play is constantly being redefined, as something which is a prelude to work, something which interferes with work, as a form of learning. Play is something done at particular times, and seldom if ever by teachers. Play is what young children do; work is done for the teacher.

Children begin to develop an attitude towards work which derives from these impressions, and begin to assume that it is those comparatively brief periods of 'work' that most matter. This also means that children accept that waiting for the next task to be presented to them is an essential part of school. Children wait while the classroom is organized, and sometimes look for things to do, volunteering help—'Shall I shut the door'?—or doing some covert reading or talking. Waiting includes keeping an eye on the teacher to be ready for that movement when she gives an instruction to which they have to pay attention. Children wait for tasks without questioning the purpose of what they are doing. The setting of tasks and the creation of order does not imply that the children are learning in every moment.

Given the extraordinarily difficult demands on primary school teachers, and given the traditionally bare resources devoted to one classroom and thirty children, it is not surprising that the experience of some children can be as seemingly purposeless as in the picture just given. But the real problem for the many creative and talented classteachers is to harness a sense of purpose both in individual children and in the schools as a whole.

Primary teachers have not been helped by some of the mythologies about school. Many of the associations fostered by the Plowden report seem gratifying, but have not really enabled teachers to define their own sense of purpose. We know about the capacities of children, but cannot assume that their talents will reveal themselves the moment they are given the opportunity. The Plowden report emphasized the need to nurture the personal growth of individual children rather than more formal aspects of learning, and directed attention away from the school to the child's own environment. But this was not a precise shift towards the involvement of parents, or towards planning specific ways in which those outside school could help children. Classrooms remained the same; they were only seen differently. Such optimism about childhood innocence meant that teachers were not supposed to be dogmatic about knowledge, and could not impose on the children. Instead they were to let children acquire knowledge from personal experience, and to create conditions in which they could do so. Such an account necessarily simplifies some of the arguments from the Plowden report but it does suggest that at the core of the report lay the belief that the role of the primary teacher was more to support than to direct. The teachers should provide a rich environment in which children would flourish of their own accord.

The problem with such a Plowdenesque view of primary education is that it does not define the purpose or the role of the teachers, or, indeed, the nature of what the children are supposed to learn.

The popularity of the Plowden report gave impetus to the idea that social and emotional development was more important than intellectual achievement. There was bound to be a reaction against such a perceived position, and this then led to a polarization of the views about the purpose of primary schools, especially in the early years. In simple terms schools are supposed either to provide a secure environment for learning or teach the children to do well academically. The desire to lay down a centralized curriculum, with objectives of achievement in terms of knowledge, which can be tested, is to be seen, since the 1978 Primary Survey, as an almost inevitable reaction. The wish to order what proportion of time should be spent on 'core' subjects and other parts of the curriculum is not just a determination to impose control but desire from outside to understand what goes on within the classroom. Individualized learning is subtle. It is easier for parents and others to understand progress in terms of subjects.

Primary schools have not been helped in articulating their sense of purpose and distinctive ethos by these conflicts between different views of their role; whether they are concerned with the process of the developing child or with the outcomes of attainment as measured against pre-set criteria.

There are many ways in which primary schools can be acknowledged for the importance of what they are doing, and be encouraged to develop the gifts of individual children, always acknowledging that their achievement could be much greater. The sense of autonomy, or freedom from imposed constraints, can be used to advantage. At best, this means that teachers can take risks, can go beyond the idea of an allotted syllabus, and explore those questions that children most want to explore, the meaning of what they are doing and the meaning of their lives in relation to others. At worst, the autonomy of the schools can lead to a lack of enthusiasm, a satisfaction with keeping children happy, making sure that there is no disturbance in the secret enclosures of the classroom.

The teacher in the traditional classroom, however, faces dangers as well as opportunities. Ostensibly, freedom from outside constraints and outside contacts can mean that there is no need to explain or articulate what is going on. Teachers rarely see other's classrooms, or visit other schools. They are nearly always in their own classroom. They are not forced by colleagues to define or analyse what they are doing. Many of the most impressive teachers, sensitive to and responding to individual children's needs, are not given an opportunity to explain what they are doing. This is one of the reasons why there is so much misunderstanding about the demands and subtleties of their role. One of the most creative uses of in-service courses is to enable teachers to work alongside others, to share their experiences and to define what they observe.

There are, however, some outside pressures which might define the work of the primary school teacher more clearly, and might, ironically, lead to greater recognition of the importance of her role. The suggestion of the Task Group on Assessment and Testing that teachers should meet to discuss both their own and national criteria in relation to each other could lead to more awareness and communication about what children are learning, and how.

Teacher appraisal is also a result of a developing concern for accountability and evaluation; firstly for institutions and then for individuals. It could mean little more than a diversion of resources into larger bureaucracies, with more inspectors rather than more teachers, but it could also lead to changes in which the complex skills of teaching are recognized by others. Teachers have always been evaluated, whether at an anecdotal level or in formal interviews for promotion. But judgements will become more formally based on evidence. This will require some very complex changes, with people being trained how to carry out 'clinical observation' and how to give advice. Formality in assessing the performance of the teacher also implies a commitment to staff development.

Appraisal is not just a question of removing or chastening the weaker teacher, but after diagnosing what is weak, finding the means to rectify the weakness. New forms of teacher appraisal should lead to a greater concern for the professional development of teachers, and therefore a greater awareness of what it is that makes teachers successful.When talking about 'values' it is easy to be vague, contradictory or abstract. But 'purposes' are often implicit, especially in primary schools, where the understanding of children's capacities for learning can be joined by an awareness of the intricate skills of teaching. All the subtle changes that are taking placed within the school community, from the greater involvement of parent to the demands of the national curriculum, will have an impact on the ways that teachers perform. There is a sense of inevitability about these changes because they are the result of conclusions reached from different points of view.

The recognition of the role of parents in schools, for example, is shared for opposing political reasons. From one point of view the involvement of parents means an opening up of the school, a responsiveness to society. From another it means greater accountability to the clients and the community. Teacher appraisal is seen by some as a means of making distinctions and demarcations between teachers, and removing any bad ones. By others it is seen as enhancing professional development. The role of a subject consultant might appear from one point of view the result of a standard and agreed curriculum. From another it is the manifestation of the natural enthusiasm of a teacher for her subject, whatever the subject, a specialism which conveys the excitement of the quality of learning for its own sake.

Primary school teachers constantly need to redefine their purpose because of the ambiguities with which they are confronted, between the individual 'holistic' nature of learning and the imposition of a set curriculum leading to assessment. Relying on the assumption that children are innately gifted and merely need the right environment for their gifts to manifest themselves is no more helpful than defining the body of knowledge they must possess, according to criteria worked out by age. For there is much more to what a primary school teacher does than either minding children or directing what they should learn.The paradox for teachers is the fact that the more they define their professional role, as people able to help others make better use of knowledge, the less their status is likely to be understood. The position of teachers in some countries which possess an agreed curriculum seems more secure in the eyes of the general public. But it is in the more subtle understanding of the process of education that primary schools find their central role.

As visible entities primary schools are easily recognized as distinct. But they are not uniform. There are many distinctions between the style of individual teachers and the sense of purpose in the school as a whole. The success or failure of children depends on the kinds of motivation shared by the staff and generated by them. It derives from a sense of purpose rather than a matter of what is added to the curriculum.

The purpose of primary education is not easily summarized. It is difficult to convey to those who demand that purposes are expressed in terms of curriculum outcomes symbolized by the examination system. It is also hard to express to parents and children who agree that the real purpose of education is the preparation for jobs. No amount of sentiment about schools will help either the teachers or the children. But the central concern with the individual child is a motivating factor whose potential has hardly been realized. The awareness of the role of parents, and the concern with what happens subsequently, are both helpful in defining more clearly the particular concern with the whole that primary schools convey. Drawing attention to the dilemmas should focus attention on how best we can define the means we have for helping children learn.

3 Control of the Primary Curriculum

Introduction

To those responsible for the management of the primary school curriculum, 1993 was a watershed year. Following the earlier acknowledgment by its chairman that the 'collective weight' of the statutory curriculum was too great, the agency responsible for the National Curriculum advised the Government that the statutory curriculum would have to be slimmed down; the agency responsible for the national inspection arrangements reported that those schools that had nearly covered the statutory curriculum had done so only by encouraging superficial learning in their pupils. After reporting annually research findings that the 'balanced and broadly-based' curriculum of the Education Reform Act 1988 was structurally unmanageable, I welcomed official recognition of the problem. I had some doubts, however, whether attempts at its resolution would be based on an understanding of the real problems confronting classroom teachers, heads and governing bodies. When the official review process was set in train under Dearing, the interim and final reports confirmed my fears that the main function of the Dearing review might be to save the Government's face and John Patten's neck, but not the curriculum. The real manageability problems confronting class teachers, heads and governing bodies had been avoided. The purpose of this chapter is to analyse these problems and explore ways forward in the mid- to late- 1990s.

Background

One of the paradoxes was that there would have been no manageability problem without the principles embodied in the curriculum required by the 1988 Act. These principles were that pupils were entitled to a broad and balanced curriculum of nine foundation subjects. Religious Education and Other Teaching; that expectations for pupils' attainment should be raised and embodied in nationally agreed criteria; that the curriculum should be modernized to include Science and Technology; and that assessment should serve formative purposes. It was because these principles had attracted widespread professional commitment that schools faced an unmanageable curriculum. Without them teachers could have continued their previous practice of attending to the basics of literacy and numeracy, of giving token time and status to other subjects and restricting assessment to norm-referenced tests in reading comprehension and number. The problems of curriculum manageability arose from both the legal force of, and the professional support for, the principles underlying the Government's reform of the curriculum.

None of the above is to deny that, for teachers, manageability problems were aggravated by mismanagement of the implementation of the reforms. The changes occurred too quickly, the curriculum and assessment orders were constantly revised and, in particular, there developed an unfortunate and ill-conceived language for the discourse of reform. *Level* was about the most inappropriate term for what statements of attainment represented. They stood for, according to the Task Group on Assessment and Testing Report two years' progress for a typical pupil—that is to say, they represented gradients not levels. The courtroom and the tax office were summoned up by requiring teachers to provide *evidence* and engage in *audits*. *Delivery* was seen as a mechanistic term for the delicate interchanges thought to characterize teaching and learning, although I think we could reclaim the metaphor's value by invoking the maternity hospital. Most importantly, with the exception of Coopers and Lybrand Deloitte, no-one took into account the time which it would take teachers to prepare, implement and assess the statutory curriculum. Irritating, dispiriting and demoralizing as these were, they were mechanical matters,the consequence of generally-accepted principles being inexpertly operationalized and poorly managed by quangos, aggravated by direct and illicit interference by Ministers. The real manageability issues were more deep seated, embedded in an anachronistic system, relying almost exclusively on the generalist class teacher. As Alexander expressed it, 'the late-twentieth-century vision of primary education and the late-nineteenth-century structure for delivering them have become increasingly incongruent'.

Three problems

The problems that arose for those charged with managing the curriculum at the school level can be analysed in three discrete categories: curriculum time allocation, teacher expertise, and resources in primary schools.

The first reason for unmanageability is the apparently simple matter of *time allocation:* how much time is needed for each subject and for the whole curriculum. The problem has been commonly represented as the quart of the statutory orders and the pint pot of the teaching week. I say 'apparently simple' because, if you are sitting on a national committee inventing or revising the statutory curriculum, it must appear merely a mechanical matter. Reduce the content until the whole curriculum matches, or is slightly less than, the time available.

The second reason concerns the *task demands on class teachers* attempting to deliver the whole curriculum—most obviously the range and level of subject knowledge required, the pedagogical skills necessary, including differentiation, the sheer detail and number of Statements of Attainment, and techniques necessary for reliable assessment. These have now been seen as unrealistic demands to make upon normal classroom teachers by all save the dismal succession of Ministers of State parading before us to assert that primary teaching, especially at Key Stage 1, is not a particularly demanding job, needing for its successful performance neither graduate knowledge nor long training.

The third reason concerns *resources*. As Alexander *et al.* pointed out, primary schools are staffed less favourably than secondary schools, even when the comparison is based on only Key Stage 3, yet the range and demand of their educational activities, and therefore their staffing needs, are almost identical. When Kelly ran a computer model of Stockport's curriculum led staffing, she found that it led to staffing needs that were more-or-less identical across the five to sixteen age range.

Curriculum TIME allocation

The first difficulty faced by teachers was simple; there was too much curriculum for the time available. One reason commonly given for this was that the statutory curriculum had been invented by means of committees of subject enthusiasts who were unable to consider how their subject had to fit into the whole curriculum. As Graham, the chairman and chief executive of the National Curriculum Council at the time, noted in what might be thought of as a Pilate-like distancing commentary:

Eventual reform of the curriculum was inevitable the moment it was decided to introduce it subject by subject. The appointment of individual subject working groups guaranteed that zealots outnumbered cynics—always a dangerous thing—that no subject would be knowingly undersold. When the full enormity of the consequences became clear, complexity and over prescription became the cry of those who caused it. Nonetheless, if one had to err, it was a magnificent aberration.

There was some truth in at least the first two of these sentences, but the extent of policy error was substantially greater than Graham and Tytler allow. First, at an early stage Ministers had worked on a broad view that the Education Reform Act would create a curricular framework in which the national prescription should cover substantially less than the whole curriculum. This was because Religious Education and other important curricular areas such as health education and moral development were conceived of as lying beyond national prescription. The consultative document suggested that in schools were there was 'good practice' the National Curriculum subjects would occupy 70-80 per cent of curriculum time. Angela Rumbold was quoted in Hansard as follows:

As the legislation tries to set out the content of the curriculum...it is logical to suggest a time allocation for subjects within the school week or term. During the consultation period we discussed how to achieve what is required in the core and foundation subjects within a given time and whether the time allocated to them should be 60 per cent during the primary years.

It is uncertain how the discussions referred to

by Mrs. Rumbold progressed, but they appear to have been short-lived. For in the event, the working groups were given notional time allocations for their subjects, as shown in Table 1.

Three implications arose for curriculum management from the notional time allocations in this table. The most important is that they represented an error that was to have disastrous effects as the curriculum was implemented. The notional time for English and Mathematics combined, was dramatically lower than was conventionally provided by primary teachers, according to every study that had examined time allocations in the post-war period. A summary covering much of the relevant research in the last fifteen years showed that 50 per cent of time was typically given to English and Mathematics, excluding their application to other subjects.

Empirically, the phenomenon of 50 per cent of time on these two subjects—what we might call the 'basic instinct' in the primary curriculum—is firmly established. Indeed, a study by Meyer *et al.* which is an examination of official elementary and primary curricula world-wide across this century until the late 1980s, argues that the phenomenon has been a global constant—irrespective of region, political economy or state of development. They show that the national language take one-third and Mathematics one-sixth of official curricula: one-tenth of time is allocated to each of Science, Social Studies, Aesthetic Subjects, Physical Education and to Moral / Social / Religious

Development. In the primary curriculum the basic instinct rules, OK?

The second point refers to the time available for the whole curriculum. It relates to 'evaporated time', a term coined in a professional development programme and used by Campbell and Neill to indicate time technically available for teaching but used for non-cognitive purposes such as supervising children changing for PE, moving them from one location in the school to another, lining up and clearing away. It is important because it is assumed to be available for teaching, but the studies referred to above that took account of this time by excluding it from teaching time, showed that something between 22 per cent of teaching time evaporates in this way, the amount depending upon the age of the pupils and the physical layout and size of the school and the methodology of time analysis. In general, younger pupils and those in open-plan settings experience more evaporated time. It occurs in small units of time in any one day, but in Campbell and Neill's research, based on time logs of over 3000 days from over 300primary teachers, the average evaporated time per week was calculated at nearly two hours per week, equivalent to nearly 10 per cent of the teaching time available and equal to the notional time allocated for at least one of the non-basic subjects, in the National Curriculum.

Thomas argues sharply that the view I have just outlined represents a top-down 'university' view of subjects and that the activities involved in evaporated time could be used for cognitive goals:

getting a sense of place, number bonding, etc., as well as important social goals such as tying shoe laces, learning social rules, etc. This is true but it is empirically unlikely that this is how the teachers generally use or plan to use such time.

A third point, made 8in the classroom observational studies is that subjects given large amounts of time are the ones in which lowest proportions of pupil time on task were observed. For example, Alexander's study showed pupils distracted for 21 per cent of time on average in all curriculum areas with 26 per cent and 23 per cent of time spent in English and Mathematics, respectively distracted, but only 13 per cent and 10 per cent distraction in Music and PE respectively. We cannot translate time formally allocated, directly into time spent by pupils on learning the subject. Moreover, as in all human activities, with the possible exception of sexual intercourse, the time spent does not necessarily reflect quality. Long hours spent on repetitive computation exercises do not necessarily mean challenging learning for bright pupils any more than do long hours spent by low-attaining pupils on tasks too difficult for them.

Nonetheless, the conclusion from the research findings on time showed no general problem in primary classrooms about the adequacy of time being spent on teaching and learning the two basic subjects. Evidence after the introduction of the National Curriculum suggested that little had changed, with Campbell and Neill showing 51 per cent and 49 per cent of time devoted to the basics.

The reasons for this state of affairs are three well-known ones. First, as Ashton's research showed, drawing on a national sample of 1500 primary teachers in the early 1970s, the highest curricular priority was given to the basic skills of Reading, Oracy, Mathematics and Writing. Art. PE, Music, Sex Education, Science and Technology and a second language were given low priority. A follow-up study by Ashton with a less representative sample at the end of the 1970s, showed, if anything, higher priority placed on Mathematics and formal language competence. Thus, commitment to the basics has always been at a premium in the professional culture. Second, parents and governors place highest curricular priority on the basics also, as Thomas's investigation of London schools showed, and the Government has required greater teacher accountability to parents and governors. Third, there has been a long tradition, stretching was back before 1988, of formal testing focused on Reading Comprehension and Mathematics, a tradition reinforced by National Curriculum assessment arrangements, though it is now slightly broadened by the inclusion of Science in the core. Such testing washes back into curriculum priorities. The basic instinct is sustained and reinforced by the workplace culture in primary schools.

Thus it becomes startlingly clear that the National Curriculum in primary schools, introduced by a series of Secretaries of State who had constantly banged on about the need to get back to basics and to raise standards of literacy and numeracy, put in place policy guidance designed to reduce the time typically spent by primary teachers on the basics, and especially on English, where the astonishing reduction of about one-third of existing time was proposed. With respect to time allocations, the policy guidance outstripped the practice in the schools for liberality and breadth. It offered a fundamentally different concept and ideology of curriculum balance.

Let me make the point most sharply. The guidance given to the working group devising the English curriculum was such as to encourage infant teachers to reduce the time they typically spent teaching children to read and write from about seven hours to little over four hours a week. No wonder there was widespread stress at Key Stage 1 with infant teachers accurately reporting that, against their own professional judgment, they were having to reduce the time on hearing children read in order to fit in everything else.

As if to confirm this interpretation of the general policy, the National Curriculum Council issued guidance on planning the Key Stage 2 curriculum in which three presumably recommended case studies of school planning were provided: two of them (year 6 and 5 classes) suggested that the basics should be planned to occupy 41 per cent and 37.5 per cent of curriculum time respectively. The Year 5 class plan was developed into a yearly programme in which Mathematics and English occupy 316 out of the

846 hours available, some 37 per cent of curriculum time in their terms. Schools are urged by the NCC to review the exercise, including reviewing whether the time allocations are appropriate. In this context, it is interesting, but confusing, to see that in the summer *Update* from the NCC, the curriculum planning in a Coventry primary school was celebrated; it initially used a plan which involved only 40 per cent of time on basics, but after trilling, it changed to 50 per cent.

There was thus built into the curriculum at national level a four-pronged problem for every primary school: too much planned prescription overall; too much content in the statutory orders for each subject: not enough flexibility to allow for evaporated time; a pretence or assumption that there would be more time available for the non-basics than there was in actuality.

Task demands on teachers

The task demands placed on class teachers by the National Curriculum have been analysed by Thomas, who shows that in the slimmed down curriculum, teachers at Key Stage 2 had to be familiar with about 500 statements of attainment, detailed and confusingly presented programmes of study, poorly defined cross-curricular themes and religious education. In addition they would have to posses subject knowledge in the ten subjects up to about Level 6, or to be able to differentiate the planning, teaching and assessment across at least 4 levels or the curriculum in each subject. To achieve all this they would need to be the curricular school equivalent of Albert Einstein. Marie Curie and Linford Christie rolled into one. The evidence about subject expertise sometimes takes a narrow view of the concept but the review of research by Bennett and Summers suggests that there are serious deficiencies in individual primary teachers' understandings, especially but not exclusively in the science and technology areas. Graduate students training for primary teaching provide no greater reasons for being sanguine, if those studied by Bennett and Carre are typical. They brought with them to their PGCE courses misunderstandings of everyday phenomena, such as the energy in a sledge moving down a hill, the explanations for night and day, and basic arithmetic competencies such as expressing $18 as a percentage of $120. Bennett and Carre's research used tests in Mathematics, English and Science based on National Curriculum levels 4, 5 and 6, and Assessment of Performance Unit (APU) tests. In some of these latter, the top 20 per cent of primary pupils scored higher than the average of the PGCE students. Technically, of course, the curriculum demands are placed on the whole school rather than the individual teacher, but in practice for the medium term further, most teachers will remain responsible for teaching most of the curriculum for the pupils in their class. Given the research findings, Alexander, Rose and Woodhead's assertion that, 'Teachers must possess the subject knowledge which the statutory orders require' sounds like a plea of desperation. A major management issue therefore becomes how the specialist expertise in the whole staff group can be deployed to extend the work of class teachers, with the overarching purpose that, as Richards argued, such deployment should 'support not undermine' the class teacher's role.

The resourcing of primary schools

The previous two problems for manageability apply to all schools irrespective of location, size or other factors. Resource issues affect schools differentially, depending upon funding formulae, school size or pupil characteristics. There is however one key resource issue—the level of staffing. The disadvantage for primary schools of historic staffing allocations has been acknowledged for almost a decade, although the difficulty of translating the acknowledgment into staffing resources has been enormous, particularly since the acknowledgment occurred in a period of public expenditure restraint. Nonetheless, if primary schools are to develop more specialist approaches to the curriculum, if class size should rarely exceed 30, and if teachers are to have some time free of class teaching in the school day; if, in short, the schools are to be enabled to implement the National Curriculum without stress and overload remaining a chronic feature of teachers' work, some improvement in the resourcing of schools is required. Acknowledgment is no longer enough. The funding formula at local level and the approval of schemes of devolved management at national level will need to be based on realistic assessment of the work activities now required of teachers in modern primary schools. Without the development of such national or local policies there will remain constraints on the extent to which the curriculum reform policy can succeed.

The dearing review

For the management of primary schools, the Dearing review's interim report appeared to hold out seductive promises to make the curriculum manageable by sliming it down.

In terms of the analysis provided so far, however, it was limited to the issue of time allocations, and my evaluation of Dearing start form this recognition; the review had nothing to say about subject expertise or resourcing, perhaps more fundamental problems than time allocation. Even the restricted problem-solving of the final report is a sleight of hand in respect of the 'curricular arithmetic' of time allocations, according to Alexander and Campbell. Dearing's approach was to allocate 20 per cent of curriculum time for discretionary use by the school and to free two weeks of the school from any curricular prescription, and then to offer guidance on time allocation for the remaining time, viz for 80 per cent of thirty-six weeks. In discussing his own arithmetic, Dearing acknowledged that it was difficult to apply it to apply it to primary schools: 'Specific time will have to be set aside for work in English, but the full 30 per cent (KSI) and 25 per cent (KS2) does not have to be found in addition to time given to other subjects.' Perhaps too defensively Dearing added, "This is not sleight of hand; it is a statement of fact based on the realities of teaching expressed by teachers'. His own arithmetic was presented in a table in para, 4.20. I give it above, with the bracketed figures referring to cross-curricular application, and therefore not counted in the total. I have added percentages based on the total annual hours of 612 and 675 for which national prescription was envisaged, and these percentages appeared to reflect the historic practices of teachers, at least at KSI, with about 50 per cent given over to the basics. There was however an assumed reduction in the proportion given to English at KS2. Alexander and Campbell however provide an alternative arithmetic, based on the overall time, not just the 80 per cent. Their arithmetic is given.

Expressed this way, Dearing appears to have rendered almost a quarter of the school curriculum year discretionary, and therefore to have solved the manageability problem. However, as Alexander and Campbell show, there are five reasons why this has not really happened. First, the percentages for English and Mathematics are dramatically lower then previous or current practice, and time will have to be taken from the allegedly discretionary time to restore the basic instinct of 50 per cent time on them. Second, there is no educational cr research-based justification for Dearing's assertion that as primary children become older they need less time on English. The DES Primary Staffing Survey found 27 per cent allocated to English in the junior stage, and while it is obvious that the nature of English at KS1 is different from that at KS2, it is not clear why is should take less time. Nor has it done so in practice. Third, time on science has been reduced from what was previously proposed as necessary and the 10-15 per cent of time that was actually needed for the science curriculum. Fourth, national testing remains focused on the core subjects, pressing in on school management to ensure that teachers give priority to them in time allocation. Allowing for evaporated time. Alexander and Campbell calculated that all discretionary time would have to go to the core. Fifth, the time remaining for the other subjects will be inadequate, especially for those that are time consuming, such as PE, Music, Art and Technology. Sixth, without good reason, excessive time has been set aside for RE. As a consequence, the only way the curriculum will become manageable is if it is recognized for what it is, underneath the Dearing rhetoric a return to the elementary curriculum of the basic and RE updated with some Science and Information Technology. But manageability will have been gained at the expense of breadth and balance. As Alexander and Campbell comment: 'The elementary school curriculum is alive and well and living in Dearing.' Thus Dearing's solution to the curriculum manageability problem was to draw on a mechanistic arithmetic which enabled him to pretend to retained commitment to the broad and balanced curriculum, while leaving in place all the old pressures in the primary school culture to concentrate on the basics at the expense of other subjects. As I argued above, the issue of time allocation is only one part of the problem, but even this aspect has been mishandled. What are the implications for the management of schools?

Management implications

This stage of the argument is based on two assumptions about the relationship between a national quango and individual schools. National quangos are not good at details, and have little competence in respect of the curriculum organization of individual schools. For example, within the space of nine months the National Curriculum Council and the School Curriculum and Assessment Authority could not even agree on the simple technical matter of how many hours per year should be considered as available for instruction. Second, as Thomas pointed out, the National Curriculum was established by reference to the best practice in each subject. To be 'best' or even good at everything is not common in individual human beings or their institutions so that there was and is a certainly that virtually and schools would, to some degree, fail to meet the statutory requirements. He added that 'Schools in other countries commonly fail to meet the requirements of their national curricula'.

If these two assumption are confirmed, the first lessons for school management are that it is in the individual school, not a national agency, that will create a curriculum that can be made to work for the school concerned; and that concern to cover the whole curriculum will have to be tempered by consideration of quality and standards in pupils learning. This latter goal might be more readily arrived at by the school establishing its curricular priorities than by attempting to deliver every statutory prescription equally well. It was, after all, the quango charged with the inspection of schools that first made clear that coverage had been achieved only at the cost of depth in pupil learning. To restore confidence in their own professional judgment, it may first be necessary for teachers to lose faith in the ability of the national agencies to manage the curriculum implementation process sensibly. Dependency on external forces is as counter productive for the whole school staff as it is for the head and is likely to reduce rather than increase empowerment and accountability. On this basis six possible ways forward may be identified, though each will be contested by some teachers because of the value assumptions it contains.

Time allocation

First, in respect of time allocation, there is the possibility that much more of the teaching of English and Mathematics than currently might be planned, delivered and assessed through their application to other subjects. This is a position advocated for at least fifteen years by HMI, but has been found problematic in practice. The problem is not helped by the framing of the curriculum in single subjects, nor by the tendency for mathematics and English schemes to be subject-specific. It is a good example of how a staff would have to have confidence as HMI had, that standards in the basics would improve by their being applied to other subjects. Unfortunately, it may be easier for staff in schools where pupils already have high achievement to develop such confidence than for staff where pupils appear to need substantial amounts of time on basic skills.

Second, schools might consider the use of homework as part of their overall policy, especially perhaps at KS2. If there is shortage of time for English, part of the solution might be to cease to consider the pupils' curriculum time as synonymous with the timetabled school day. Successful experience at SI1 with parental partnerships provides exemplars for developing similar approaches at KS2. Some opposition might be raised by those who would see such a systematic approach to homework as increasing the disadvantages of pupils who live in unsupportive families or physical conditions unconductive to doing homework. School-based provision for facilities for doing homework, while a contradiction in terms, might go some way to mitigating the difficulties, though at a cost in staff supervision time.

A third solution to the problem of curriculum time might be to extend the school day, week or year. This is clearly sensible for these schools who currently spend less than the minimum expected weekly hours on instruction. It will be opposed on grounds of workload and of inappropriateness in rural areas where pupils have to travel long distances. It might also be surmised that while the current assessment and testing policy remains in place, any extra time would be devoted to the core and thus not release time for the non-core, which is the problem.

Subject expertise

It has been suggested that a solution to teachers' lack of confidence and competence in subject expertise could be remedied by a greatly expanded In-service training programme along lines similar to the DES twenty-day courses. This is obviously true, assuming that the courses are effective, and that their effects are long-lived, an assumption that Bennett and Summer's review of research questions in part. However, the problem for primary schools is that extensions of In-service training programmes are also extensions of the times when teachers have to be away from school and their class, so that a substantial programme of In-service Training in the school day may have disadvantages for pupil learning where schools do not have access to good quality supply cover.

A second possibility lies in suggestions that schools should deploy their staff in ways that enable their subject expertise to be exploited more effectively to the benefit of the school as a whole, whether as specialists, semi-specialists or as coordinators. Again, within limits, this might offer gains to some schools, especially those with staffing allocations that permit some flexibility of deployment. For most schools, however there is almost no flexibility, and, as school size reduces, the range of subjects in which there is staff expertise also reduces.

A third possibility is that more use should be made of class texts in which the teachers can have confidence that the intellectual content is reliable, freeing them to concentrate more upon planning for how pupils may learn more effectively from the texts. There may be some reluctance in the profession to the purchase of texts for whole classes, since it is seen as at odds with concepts of good practice which stress learning from first hand experience, building on pupils' interests, and practical investigation. While recognizing that purchasing class texts will not solve all problems, I detect a note of educational political correctness in such opposition, perhaps influenced by past images of whole classes sitting reading class textbooks at the same pace, each pupil being asked to read aloud with the rest of the class following. The way texts are used with primary classes is obviously an important matter, but the adoption of good quality class texts would be the quickest way of helping class teachers cope with both the cognitive demands of the whole curriculum and the time demands of preparing all learning materials for their pupils. There is something puritanical in a professional culture which implies that the virtuous teacher is the one who prepares every worksheet herself. I would even go further and suggest that one of the few ways that a national quango could make itself useful to teachers would be to issue 'kitemarks' to texts to indicate that the statutory orders were accurately and adequately covered by them and that there were useful assessment activities integrated into them. This is, politically speaking, quite different from requiring that schools use one particular prescribed text.

Resources

Little useful can be added about the formulate by which, externally, resources are allocated to schools, beyond what has been argued earlier. On the internal allocation of the resources when allocated, one further point needs to be raised. In most primary schools lack of time, especially lack of time in the school day, has been a major obstacle to effective delivery of the curriculum. Yet Campbell and Neill showed that teachers spent about eighteen house a week teaching, and between five and six hours a week on low level routines, such as mounting displays, supervision, moving pupils round the school, registration, and collecting dinner money, etc. Where teacher had more time with a non-teaching assistant, they tended to spend more, not less time on such routines, probably because of the 'collaborative cultures' operating in them. Yet there is something unsettling about the picture of teachers naming lack of time as the main obstacle to achieving the cognitive objectives of the curriculum while spending so much time on non-cognitive routines. Given that teacher time is the most valuable and most expensive resource available to a school, it is worth the management of the school exploring the advantages of re-thinking the use of time of all adults on the staff of the school, to see whether the non-teaching assistants' time might be used imaginatively to free up teachers' time. On a more radical analysis, the automatic replacement of a departing teacher by another one rather than by a part-time teacher with more extensive non-teaching support, may need exploration.

4 The Primary Child and the Teacher's Training

Training and teaching: causality or correspondence?

In this and the two chapters following we shall explore the formal basis of the teacher's knowledge of children, curriculum and pedagogy - the course of initial training - which legitimises the claims about 'the whole child' and 'the whole curriculum' in which primary ideology and practice are grounded and which we examined.

I use 'formal' advisedly. Professional groups validate their professional claim by reference to 'expert' knowledge, supposedly hard-won and rigorously tested, but few people are naive enough to believe that in a job as complex as teaching such formal training provides the sole resource for subsequent professional thought and action. Experience plays a substantial part. 'On the job', teachers develop skills and insights through constant interaction with children; they come to recognise patterns, commonalities and recurrences in behaviours, situations and problems and thereby develop habits of diagnosis and response whose practical effectiveness they can confidently demonstrate. similarly, to an extent perhaps not sufficiently recognised, teachers draw on their pre-training experience; for, uniquely among professionals, they are engaged in a process with which they have already been involved, continuously and unremittingly, since the age of five or earlier. Their teacher training course is but a brief part of this total, cumulative educational experience and the latter, as much as the specifics of the one to four year training course, shapes the view of the educational process and its purposes within which they operate as teachers. It is a commonplace that many young teachers teach as they were taught in school rather than as they were urged to teach in college. Significantly too, teachers themselves display ambivalent attitudes towards initial training. In the context of debate and negotiation about salary and status the teacher is a 'trained professional' in possession of expertise denied to all but those who submit themselves to the rigours of Certificate, BEd, or PGCE. But in everyday discourse, good teachers are 'born, not made' and that same expert knowledge may be dismissed as 'irrelevant' theory.

The truth is that it is empirically impossible to isolate initial training from earlier, contemporaneous or subsequent experience for the purposes of demonstrating its precise impact on the way a teacher performs in the classroom. It seems sensible to assume that it does have an impact, but to avoid the extremes of the grandiose strategic claim prepared for negotiation with Burnham on the one hand, and the dismissiveness of teacher folklore and staffroom conventional wisdom on the other. Instead, two hypotheses can be supported. One is that by incorporating in its emphasis on certain sorts of knowledge and skill particular views of the teaching role, the nature and needs of young children, the initial training course tends to facilitate some lines of subsequent professional development and to discourage others. Second, initial training influences subsequent development as much by what it omits or does badly as by what it treats positively; or, to use for the sake of convenience some mild jargaon, a course may 'de-skill' as well as 'skill'. This latter point is particularly apposite in the present context, given that we have seen how primary ideology may relate to professional insecurity. the ideology, it will be recalled, is most strongly focused and most forcibly expressed in relation to those aspects of primary teaching where empirical study shows the greatest weakness.

What we can show, therefore, is not firm evidence of behavioural casuality - element *x* in initial training produces action *y* in the classroom - so much as a succession of positive and negative correspondences between training and subsequent practice which are sufficiently pervasive and exact as to leave little doubt about a causal relationship of some sort, albeit diluted by the power of experience, circumstance and contingency, and mediated through each individual's unique combination of personality, intellect and worldview.

Primary teacher training: background

To provide a framework for the analysis which

follows it is necessary at this point to give a brief resume of the overall structures and contexts of courses.

There are two main routes into primary teaching, the four year BEd and the one year PGCE. The former is a post 'A' level undergraduate course and the latter, self-evidently, is taken by graduates in subjects which could equally well lead to other careers.

Until recently the BEd and its predecessor the Certificate in Education constituted the major routes into teaching, but because since 1972 successive governments have used this route as the tap to regulate teacher supply the BEd/PGCE balance has now shifted. Thus in 1963 19 640 students started teacher's certificate courses, compared with a mere 3840 PGCE students, most of whom were intending secondary teachers. there followed a decade of expansion until by 1972 admissions were 37 381 and 10 365. Thereafter, delayed government panic about the declining birthrate produced the devastating cuts of the 1970s, and the mergers and closures of many colleges; until by 1980, for the first time in the history of initial training, more students entered PGCE than BEd courses. 1984-5 marked the start of a modest expansion of primary training, but one to be secured mainly through the PGCE. However, the BEd will remain for the foreseeable future the majority route into primary teaching.

More important in the context of this book's analysis, perhaps, is an awareness of the training received by those teachers by now well established in primary schools. Most were products of the 2-3-4 year route, the teacher's certificate and the BEd, and it is therefore on this route that we must necessarily concentrate in seeking to identify correspondence between initial training and primary practice.

In the recent history of the 3-4 year route, four overlapping stages are clearly discernible, which are referred to as 'Certificate', 'BEd Mark I', 'BEd Mark II' and 'BEd Mark III'.

Firstly, the rise and decline of the teacher's certificate, which expanded from two to three years in 1960, was phased out during the 1970s and enshrined the basic structural elements which have dominated discussion about teacher education ever since. That structure is generally held to be a modified version of that recommended in the McNair Report back in 1944 which in turn consolidated ideas which went back to the nineteenth century:

1. Personal' education: (a) one or more 'academic' or 'main' subjects;
2. 'Professional' education: (b) theory of education;

(c) 'curriculum' or 'professional' courses to equip the student with the content and method of the subjects he has to teach.

(d) teaching practice.

The second stage we can call BEd Mark I. Following the Robbins Report BEds were introduced at great speed. These were essentially lengthened and academicised teacher's certificate courses. Because the course was now a degree rather than a certificate, it had to be academically respectable to the validating universities and to be seen to be comparable to their other degree courses. this academic validity was seen to reside in the main subject and education theory, which were greatly strengthened, at the expense, it is now accepted, of professional studies and teaching practice.

Following increasing criticism of this course, the James Report came up with a radical alternative model, which in pure form was not implemented, but its ideas provided the basis for BEd Mark II. This was 'consecutive' and modular. Deferred student choice and flexibility were major aspirations; this was the era of the 'container revolution', of courses which students put together from a wide selection of units and modules, and which often meant that professional study and work in schools were deferred until the second or even the third of four years. By the late 1970s, deferred choice, consecutive training and modularity were running into the logistical problems attendant upon contraction, for such courses had to be large to be viable. there were other criticisms. chiefly revolving round the continued lack of sufficient professional emphasis, the perceived divorce of theory and practice and the split between subject and professional study. By now, moreover, the academic status of the BEd was no longer an issue. A large number of institutions had transferred from university to CNAA validation and alternative notions of 'degree-worthiness' had begun to be explored. Mark III BEds lasted the full four years, were usually honours only, and included serious attempts to put professional concerns at the centre of the course and at last to break down the barrier between subject and professional study.

But by that time, the early 1980s now, there were countervailing pressures. Successive HMI surveys, of primary and secondary schools had identified what were regarded as major weaknesses in serving teachers' professional expertise, above all in their curriculum knowledge. First HMI, then central government then ACSET, the teacher education advisory body - less from conviction than recognition of the irresistibility of political dogma backed by landslide election success - and finally and DES again proposed that all BEd students, whether primary or secondary, should spend half their course on main subject study in order to remedy these curricular deficiencies. The inadequacy of the models of primary curriculum, primary teaching and initial training thereby encapsulated will be discussed.

The institutional context

Courses are not disembodied artifacts but events and ideas which acquire their reality from particular institutional contexts. The majority of today's established primary teachers not only trained by the 2-3-4 year route but did so in a distinctive sort of institution, the college of education, which preserved a culture of remarkable homogeneity and historical persistence until the institutional reorganisations of the 1970s forced many of the surviving colleges into a usually reluctant alliance with mainstream higher education institutions. While the PGCE was located mainly in the universities and - until the rude advent of compulsory initial training, comprehensive schools and mixed ability teaching - prepared its students for grammar and public schools, the 3-4 year course reflected the requirements of a less prestigious tradition, that of secondary modern and primary schools. Thus the two routes embodied and reinforced the mutual exclusiveness of the two central traditions in British education: minority/elitist/academic, and mass/elementary/utilitarian. Like primary schools, the colleges' origins were humble and impoverished. Like primary schools, they acquired a substantial contrary ideology—idealist, romantic, espousing values of self-actualization, individualism and student/child-centredness.

By the 1950s and 1960s, the professionally formative years for the deputy heads, heads and advisers of the 1970s and 1980s, the college ethos was predominantly one, in Taylor's often-quoted words, of 'social and literary romanticism':

Partial rejection of pluralism: suspicion of the intellect and the intellectual; a lack of interest in political and structural change; a stress upon the intuitive and the intangible, upon spontaneity and creativity... a hunger for the satisfactions of interpersonal life within the community and the small group, and a flight from rationality.

The extent to which this incorporates caricature is debatable, but when one considers the institutions into which most of the products of these colleges went—primary schools—the correspondence is irresistible. Taylor was writing about a 1950s/1960s college; he could equally have been anticipating some 1970s/1980s primary schools.

Specific manifestations and echoes of these values will continue to emerge from our discussions. We turn now, however, from general background to the first of several specific aspects of initial training; the means whereby it seeks to generate that 'understanding of children' required for primary class teaching and pre-eminent in the class teacher's professional claim.

The contribution of psychology and sociology of education

In most post-war teacher education courses the intending teacher's capacity to understand and relate to children has been seen as the virtually exclusive concern of two elements:

(a) *academic* - courses in what until the 1960s were termed 'principles of education', subsequently the separate 'disciplines' of psychology and sociology of education, but more recently somewhat disguised within integrated, thematic education/professional courses;

(b) *experiential* - teaching practice and other school-based activity.

This neat exclusivity of function is characteristic of initial teacher education as a whole. The dominant post-McNair model discussed earlier demarcates not merely 'personal' and 'professional' *aspects* of the training task but personal and professional course *elements*. Little or no overlap of function is envisaged or, in terms of academic territoriality, allowed. there is assumed to be an exact correspondence, between professional attribute and course component so that each becomes the 'property' of a particular department or group of staff.

Thus 'understanding of children' is the concern not of anyone with insights to offer but of just two academic disciplines, psychology and sociology.

The lure of positivism and behavourism

Psychology is relatively well-established in initial teacher education. The MCNair Report's 'principles of education' included; physiology and physical education, psychology, 'great classical writers on education', history of the education system, and appreciation of the 'home circumstances of the pupils'. This approach lasted well into the 1960s: Taylor, Tibble, Browne and others record the dominance of the 'mother hen' - the education tutor dispensing a mixture of 'method', history of educational ideas and, above all, psychology. The 1960s witnessed the coming of age of the 'four disciplines' of education, but this strengthened the position in primary training, where the 'child development' course continued to rule supreme.

Despite this relatively long-established pre-eminence in teacher education, it must be recalled that as an academic discipline psychology is young, and sociology younger. Through a combination of empirical research and theory-generation they seek to offer descriptions and explanations of individual and collective human behaviour which must be regarded as tentative, provisional and incomplete. My first major reservation about this means of generating understanding of children is that the required sense of tentativeness and provisonality is too seldom conveyed to students. Theories and models are frequently put forward, or at least received by students, as unassailable truths about the real world, their status as such apparently confirmed by the strong positivistic orientation of a good deal of the research drawn upon and by the convenient tendency of such work to offer quantified findings.

Wilson showed how the very examination questions BEd and PGCE students were required to answer presumed their tacit acceptance of a wide range of concepts and constructs. That claim is readily substantiated. My own brief surveys of examination questions in the psychology of education approved by one validating body in 1982 produced the following not untypical examples:

1. Describe the main types of performance tests of intelligence and indicate their advantages and disadvantages over verbal tests.

2. Outline development during sensori-motor stage and discuss the importance of any one of the following concepts: object permanence; spatial relationships; causality.
3. What in view are the important influences in the formation of the self-concept?
4. Compare and contrast any two adjacent stages in piaget's theory of intellectual development.
5. What are attitudes? How can they be measured?

None of the questions invites critical appraisal: all presume a basic acceptance of ideas, hypotheses and models of sometimes considerable challengeability if not dubiousness - performance tests as means of assessment; Piagetian stage theory; particular definitions of attitudes and the assumption that they can be measured. Equally unsatisfactory, none of the questions invites application to the task of the teacher. Assuming the intending teachers duly demonstrate that they have committed the various theories, facts and arguments to memory,what then? What are they supposed to *do* with this knowledge? If it is seriously intended that it should inform their thinking about the job of teaching, why is no opportunity given for this capacity to be demonstrated? Or is it more important that they have knowledge than that they can use it?

Taking their lead from this style of questioning, essays are peppered with the catch-phrase 'Research has proved that....' without apparent regard for the need for all proof claims to be probed, for the provisionality of scientific findings.

The connection with everyday professional practice is evident. The same formulae re-emerge in much of the published work exemplified in, and in the written and spoken utterances of some serving teachers. Here, however, their linguistic hardness may be duly softened to match the gentler, familial ambience of child-centred discourse, and with the 'authority' now accorded a hushed, parent-surrogate,almost Messianic reverence: 'Piaget has shown us that...'.

In both contexts such unconditional deference, by negating the element of natural scepticism combined with informed critique vital to academic study and the proper use of academic research, effectively invalidates the latter's claim: for it is no longer knowledge—open, provisional, challengeable—but dogma.

Conversely, the students are exhorted not trust 'mere opinions', to have a higher regard for academic than common sense modes of analysis and explanation, and to prefer the 'objective' data of the social sciences to their or an experienced teacher's subjective' judgement. For example, in one widely used current teacher education text:

Understanding oneselves and others has probably always been a human preoccupation. Certainly from the time when the first written record was produced we have shown a deep interest in human and animal behaviour. Yet our ideas have been almost entirely unsystematic and unrepresentative. Even now we casually watch others or listen with prejudiced ears to conversation and from this evidence build up distorted rules of thumb about human nature.

It is of course highly probable that our 'interest in human and animal behaviour' predates written records, but that is to quibble. More problematic, it seems to me, is the implied dismissal of all but the psychologist's way of doing things as 'unsystematic', 'unrepresentative', 'casual', 'prejudiced', and 'distorted': clearly not the author's intention, but open to that interpretation by someone new to the discipline.

Thus may be generated or reinforced a basic epistemology to which the polarising of 'objective' and 'subjective', of 'fact' and 'value', of 'truth' and 'falsity', of 'knowledge' and 'belief', are fundamental. If internalised, this simplistic conceptual map is able and likely to provide signposts for a wide range of contexts: the teacher's subsequent response to educational research and theory most obviously, but also other situations in which knowledge claims are significant - record cards and diagnostic or attainment tests for example, and the wide and crucial range of claims which teachers make about children, their abilities, their potential, their home background and so on.

The other context where this epistemology bears fruit in a palpable way is the primary curriculum. Its most public and assertive face is the view of curriculum in general and knowledge in particular which we explored - for example the way a view of knowledge as brute 'fact' can be used as a justification for rejecting knowledge in any guise. Less obviously, but perhaps in the end more significant, the framework may influence the way in which different curriculum experiences are presented for the child, and the view of knowledge the child thereby acquires: art at the 'soft',, 'subjective', 'value' end of the continuum science at the 'hard', 'objective', 'fact' end.

Moreover, by according experientially derived insight lower status an initial training course misses an obvious and significant opportunity. Given that it is at the commonsense, intuitive level that the student/teacher is frequently forced to operate once under the pressure of everyday classroom circumstances, it is precisely these sorts of judgements which should be exposed and explored during initial training, with a view to refining them and making them as reliable and reflexive as possible.

However, the psychologist's rejection of such perspectives is the more emphatic for being made on methodological grounds: personal knowledge is counted not so much less significant as inadmissible. Psychology has sought to replace commonsense theories about mental processes with propositions derived from the application to human nature of the methods of the natural sciences. Pre-eminent in this methodology is the charting of observable behaviours. The 'introspective' method which seeks to uncover individuals' private knowledge, beliefs, attitudes and so on by eliciting these by word of mouth, is considered by the behaviourist majority to be inconsistent with the scientific claim. Thus because by the canons of a particular methodology such date is deemed inaccessible, as the object of study it ceases to be of interest.

This raises broader issues concerning the historical development of psychology - its origins in the philosophy of mind, the late 19th century rejection of mind in favour of 'scientific' study of the brain and the central nervous system, the consequent issue of the distinctiveness of psychology vis-a-vis neurology and physiology, and the continuity of the behaviourist/introspectionist debates. Such issues are beyond the scope of this book, but what is important for teachers and teacher educators is an awareness of the consequences for the way their task is defined in initial training. For teachers are not neuro-surgeon: their main focus of concern is that elusive entity, which causes psychologists such difficulty, the human mind. Despite this, and paradoxically, psychology is granted a virtual monopoly of the topic and the monopoly is usually exercised by adopting the behaviorist position, which psychologists themselves acknowledge to be controversial and challengeable. Alternative perspectives on children which would complement the portrayal of the behaviourist psychologist - from literature, drama, philosophy and pre-eminently, everyday discourse - are explicitly rejected.

Apart from its tendency to impoverish the teacher's professional development and classroom thought, this monopoly reveals the extent to which the view of teaching as science has pervaded academic and professional opinion, even including groups—like literature teachers and tutors - who might be expected to be more resistant. Perhaps, as academics so often do, they fail to make the connection between the claim that the arts offer unique and profound insights into the human condition and the obvious fact that teaching itself is nothing if not concerned with that condition.

Three provisos must, however, be expressed, lest it be thought that this chapter's discussion stems basically from an anti-psychology standpoint.

The first is that the teacher education community as a whole, rather than its psychologists alone, have to take responsibility for excluding alternative sources of insight into children in general and into their mental processes in particular. There has been large-scale connivance at this needless impoverishment of the training process.

Second, I am arguing for courses as a whole to incluae addition perspectives not for psychologists to do what artists do. Psychology is psychology and literature is literature. Each represents a distinctive way of making sense of our situation. As Hebb, an uncompromising objectivist and behaviorist, himself argues:

The other way of knowing about human

beings is the intuitive artistic insight of the poet, novelist, historian, dramastiser and biographer. This alternative to psychology is a valid and deeply penetrating source of light on man, going directly to the heart of the matter..I challenge anyone to cite a scientific psychological analysis of character to match Conrad's study of Lord Jim, or Boswell's study of Johnson, or Johnson's of Savage...Trying to make over Science to be simultaneously scientific and humanistic...falls between two stools. Science is the servant of humanism, not part of it'. Combining the two ruins both.

The third proviso is that the psychology component of teacher education courses, particularly until, in the mid 1970s, it began to be taught by graduates with a board psychological training, may have been singularly unrepresentative of the parent discipline. It might, for example, over-emphasis Skinnerian behaviourism or developmental psychology; it might neglect study of the unconscious mind or of the social dimension of behaviour. It might fail to develop in students a proper consciousness of the extent to which a psychological model is a metaphor for behaviour, not the behaviour itself nor ever necessarily a particularly accurate representation of it. Above all it might fail to convey the necessary sense of psychology, as of every discipline, as variegated, contentious and changing.

The dominance of developmental approaches

The extent to which psychology of education courses directly reinforce the 'sequential developmentalism' element in primary ideology, which—drawing on King and others—provides a good example of several of the points above, particularly those concerning distortion in content and methodological oversimplification. The central theme or core of such courses has traditionally been a chronological treatment of child development. Here 'development' is conceived as a matrix with norms for ages and stages providing one axis and various categories of human development—'intellectual', 'social', 'emotional', 'moral', 'physical' etc.—the other. This developmental matrix, open to fundamental criticism as it is provides a basic, widely accepted structure for primary discourse, curriculum planning and pupil assessment: the firmly fixed reference points on an otherwise shifting and undifferentiated map.

It is usually well understood that the ages attached to stages postulated by Piaget are approximate, and that the inevitability of the sequence and the state-independent processes and mechanisms of cognitive development—equilibration, assimilation, accommodation—are more significant than any inferred chronology. Yet it is notable that in student essays, as in professional discourse and teachers, books and curriculum materials,the stages as such feature more prominently than the stage-independent theory, despite the fact that an understanding of the latter is essential to using the undoubted insights of Piagetian theory to promote or accelerate learning. A Piagetian approach to HMI's concept of 'match', for example, would demand that children encounter learning tasks which are slightly, but not excessively, more complex than their present understanding, and that without this element of 'stretching' the disequilibration necessary for learning will not be produced. Where students or teachers perceived development in terms of states rather than processes they will tend to wait for learning to occur 'spontaneously' or 'naturally' rather than seek as teachers to advance it, on the grounds that the child has to be 'ready'.

Educational 'failure': the child and the teacher

Just as the dominance of developmentalism in everyday practice is matched by the dominance of the developmental 'matrix' in educational psychology courses, so the traditional fare of sociology of education courses corresponds strongly with another element in professional discourse, the family and home as the prime or even sole causes of the child's difficulties or failures at school. Until the early to mid-1970s sociology of education courses were dominated by the issue of the effect of family and social-class factors on the child's attainment at school. Early studies of streaming pointed the way to the possibility that the school itself might be a contributory factor in the under-achievement of working-class children, but research on class-related socialisation practices, parental attitudes, language and so on tended to swamp such relatively slender evidence. Only with the 'new' sociology of education, with its two-pronged, ideologically committed concern to explore first the cultural loading of the school and its curriculum in favour of certain groups of pupils and, second, the nature of everyday classroom life, did alternatives to the family/home deficit model present themselves with much credibility. A substantial literature concerning the effect of teacher expectations on pupil performance, teacher constructs and typifications, classroom interaction and teaching styles, now permits a more balanced appraisal of the relative impact of family and school, parents and teachers, on the child's educational career. Some of this work was referred.

The shift, however, is recent, and everyday primary discourse, in as far as it is demarcated and to some extent controlled by senior members of the profession such as heads and advisers, still appears to display fairly unreserved affiliation to family/home theories; certainly the confident professional assertions about 'good' and 'poor' parents and homes are part of the essential fabric of both staffroom discussion and pupil record cards.

What will be worth monitoring is the extent to which the 'new' sociology of education produces a discernible shift in the way children's learning difficulties or lack of motivation are explained as students of the 1970s gain headhips in the 1980s and 1990s and seek to influence their school's 'philosophies'. If, however, the family/home background theory is such an indispensable element in professional ideology as I have argued - in that, for the weaker teacher in particular, it is fundamental to the preservation of his self-esteem we can anticipate little movement overall.

Understanding the child, or understanding the teacher?

Theories of child development and educability, it will be apparent, not only have ideological potential but need to be simplified, and perhaps even distorted, to achieve that potential. Thus, as I have suggested, Piagetian theory may be interpreted as confirming a doctrine of 'readiness' rather than as challenging the teacher's ingenuity to provide the child with appropriately structured and sequenced learning experiences. Similarly, the complexity and tentativeness of, say, Bernstein's work on language and social structure may be ignored in preference for gross polarisations of 'restricted' and 'elaborated' codes which may confirm a student's or teacher's existing cultural stereotypes and prejudices. Both theories exemplified can be invoked to justify low expectations of children - on the 'grounds' of age, or of social class. In fact, much of the theoretical material regarded as indispensable in initial training is intrinsically extremely elusive and difficult to understand, let alone to apply, and especially so for the 18-21 year old with neither professional experience of schools and children nor a background of introductory study in the social sciences. However, its misinterpretation could be reduced or offset if the typificatory process which it appears to reinforce were itself the object of scrutiny on initial training courses. But it is a characteristic of mainstream education courses in initial training that, more recent sociology and social psychology perspective apart, they tend to devote little attention to the teacher as such.

This particularly true of psychology of education courses: an examination of student texts and course syllabuses will reveal that most deal not so much with the psychology of *education* as with the psychology of the *child*, and that child's education is treated only in so far as it can be conceived independently of the person who is its chief architect, the teacher. The child emerges with an identity shaped by a combination of heredity and environment, having characteristics which are given and immutable. There is little or no psychological analysis of adults in general or teachers in particular; nor of the teacher's contribution to that classroom character of the child which serves as the basis for the teacher's appraisal of him or her. The child's actions are presented, if only by default, as independent of the teacher's; a conception of the child is encouraged which is somehow independent of the person, the teacher, who does the conceiving.

These tendencies can be illustrated by comparing two recent psychology of education textbooks.

Child's *Psychology and the Teacher* focuses almost exclusively on the learner: motivation, attention, perception, learning theory, concept formation, language and thought, intelligence, creativity, personality, handicap and so on. Though the analysis is sufficiently comprehensive for it to be applied, sometimes, to teachers as well as to children, that connection is not really made: tacitly, the teacher emerges as well motivated, perceptive, able to learn readily, conceptually advanced, linguistically sophisticated, highly and diversely intelligent, creative and of stable personality. The model is not of the interaction of minds and personalities, still less of teaching as dependent on teacher qualities as well as child attributes, but of the operating theatre: the teacher, as complete person and competent professional, works on the child's mind with the detachment of the surgeon working on the anesthetized body of the patient. Skill is presumed; the sole knowledge required is of the mental anatomy of the child.

Fontana's *psychology for Teachers* stresses in its introduction that 'no child's behaviour can be fully understood unless we study also the behaviour of others - teachers, parents, school friends - towards him', and subsequently argues that within the context of the school the teacher is the most important influence upon the child. Despite this promising beginning, and the author's reservations elsewhere about traditional psychology of education courses, twelve of the sixteen chapters are devoted to the pupil, only three to interaction and teacher-child relations, and just one to 'teacher personality and characteristics'. The latter is a brief summary of research on the behavioural characteristics of 'effective' teachers, contextualised in an acknowledgement of some of the problems involved in defining teacher effectiveness: about a page each on the teacher's emotional security, attitude, styles and classroom talk - all crucial issues but far too briefly dealt with. In addition the chapter 'Knowledge of self, which could provide a basis for the kind of analysis which is needed, though it sets out a set of propositions concerning the self-concept which could apply to all humans, applies these to the issues of self-esteem, personal maturity and identity in the pupil.

These problems are acknowledged in a recent paper by one of the authors referred to. He documents systematically the neglect in educational psychology of teacher practices and classroom process: in the *British Journal of Educational Psychology,* for example, Child records just six index entries on 'teachers' between 1930 and 1954 and 27 between 1955 and 1980, and even this increase tended to focus upon teachers apart from their classroom role, concentrating instead on supposedly 'determining' factors like personality, social origins, career expectations and so on.

Textbook writers are thus placed in something of a dilemma: they recognise a need but cannot meet it, for it is the essence of the general textbook that it draws on material which is both published and to an acceptable extent established. This is particularly the case in a discipline like psychology which is committed to the search for truths through empirical study and the accumulation of evidence. Authors, then, in doing justice to the field as it stands at the time of writing, may well recognise the omissions and anomalies in terms of what is needed, but beyond speculating on what these are they can do little to remedy them.

Worse, the lecturer and student using these books may be some way removed from the global grasp of the field which gives the writer/researcher this awareness. For them, and particularly the latter, it is what the textbook says rather than what it cannot say which is significant. In turn, this extant material forms the basis for lectures, essays and examination questions; it acquires increasing authority through familiarity and use. It comes to determine the very way in which student, lecturer and teacher may conceive of the field in question.

Moreover, in the economic climate of recent years, publishers have been increasingly reluctant to take on other than obviously marketable basic texts and course readers in education. The original or unusual is squeezed out and the second- or third-hand comes to rule supreme. Primary education has suffered particularly from the flood of edited 'readers', many of them drawing repeatedly on the same rather limited pool of 'safe' articles.

Thus, though one must not overstate the case, the public teachable, examinable face of the educational process is increasingly defined by a combination of academics' personal interests and market forces: the research which, fortuitously, happens to be feasible, interesting, fundable or available, and what publishers and entrepreneurial editors or authors see as likely to sell.

But that is to digress. As I argued earlier, 'understanding children' is an attribute not of the object of that understanding but of the teacher who claims it. The teacher will perceive a child in a particular way not only because of the sort of person that child is but because of the sort of person the teacher is. And in the primary school, we remind ourselves, the class-teacher system ensures that a child is so perceived for educational purposes for a whole year by just one person: with that much at stake it seems indefensible for initial training courses to neglect the psychology of the teacher.

Four shifts are indicated therefore. First, the inclusion, as argued, of a substantial focus on teachers and their impact on those various aspects of the learner conventionally treated as independent of them.

Second, a deeper exploration of the ways individual behaviour - whether the child's or the teacher's - can be understood in the context of, and sometimes explained as a consequence of, interaction, possibly through the use of transactional analysis techniques applies in industrial psychology and psychotherapy, as well as interaction analysis schedules and theoretical perspectives of social psychology and interactionist/phenomenological sociology. Third, a preparedness to explore the irrationality which frequently characterises human actions and interactions, not least in the classroom; the dominant psychological tradition in teacher education, as we have seen, takes the teacher's total rationality for granted and moreover imposes a sometimes over-tidy, predictive framework on the child. Fourth, just as theoretical study of children in teacher education is required to be supported by work with children in classrooms, so teachers in classrooms and above all students themselves would need to be the object of practical study. If self-exploration is now included in the training of other professional groups whose job involves the management of people and relationships, it can surely be justified in the training of teachers.

Understanding children through school experience

The second major context a course provides for developing the student's understanding of children is school experience. Again, a historical perspective on this part of the course is helpful because it character and purposes have changed in recent years, through not as radically as some current advocates of 'school-based' courses would have us believe. Forty years ago the McNair Report identified two main types of school experience, 'practical training in schools' and 'continuous teaching practice':

Practical training in schools...To provide the

concrete evidence, illustrations and examples to supplement and give point to the theoretical part of the student's training. The schools are his laboratory and the scene of his field studies. School practice of this sort should include...comparatively discontinuous periods of teaching and observations in the schools, visits, minor investigations and so on...

Continuous teaching practice... To provide a situation in which the student can experience what it is to be a teacher, that is, to become as far as possible a member of a school staff.

In 1979 a major review of school experience/ teaching practice in all CNAA-validated BEds distinguished two main types, 'intermittent' and 'block', in almost exactly the same terms as McNair, but found the former a relative novelty in many institutions, something needing further development. It was indeed a novelty, Taylor's 1969 study of teacher education reported as the norm for both Certificate and Mark I BEd courses block practices only, three in total, taking place in years 1, 2 and 3, with students given their final teaching practice grade at the beginning of year 3 and undertaking no more work in schools for a further five terms. This may seem, in retrospect, hard to defend but at the time the overriding concern of the universities—for the BEd's academic respectability—was argument enough. This arrangement ensured that professional work in general and the pressures and anxieties of teaching practice in particular were not allowed to disturb the smooth flow of what was held to matter most in the final two years of the new degree, main subject study and theoretical studies in education.

Thus, despite McNair, the history of developments in this part of the course shows three clear stages:

Stage I. The nineteenth-century 'apprenticeship' model, or what in Britain is called 'sitting by Nellie' by some teacher educators: here the student acquires most of his/her teaching competence through close association with, and imitation of, an experienced practising teacher.

Stage II. The 'teaching practice' model, where students acquire professional knowledge and skill in the training institution, then apply or 'practise' these during extended periods in school, watched over by the experienced teacher whose class they take over, and visited once a week or so by their college/university tutor.

Stage III. The 'school-based study' or 'school experience' model, where the school becomes not only a place to practise teaching, to demonstrate what one can do and to be assessed, but also a place to learn, to observe, to study and to experiment; to carry out specific tasks of observation, working with small groups of children, working alongside experienced teachers, undertaking small-scale inquiries, analysing at first hand how children develop, how they learn, the different styles of teaching used, how children respond to these,

> their impact on children's learning ... and so on. The school here is perhaps the central resource and arena for the student's professional education and it follows that the close relationship of theoretical and subject studies with specific school-based activities is essential. What is viewed as the minimum precondition is partnership between teachers and trainers and a mutual exchange of ideas and personnel between schools and training institutions.

The latter is the model most earnestly being explored at present, and to some extent with government support: the government at the time of writing want more school experience than hitherto, and a greater involvements by serving teachers in initial training—in selecting students for entry to courses and in assessing their teaching competence.But it must be clear that the reality of 'partnership' is less easy than the rhetoric: it requires very fundamental shifts in traditional attitudes towards teacher education by both teachers and trainers, and involves changes in structure and procedures at the institutional level and between schools and colleges/ universities.

Clearly, whatever the espoused objective of school experience, students will gain some view of children simply by virtue of interacting with them. This applies equally when the acquisition of such experiential understanding is explicitly valued and when more limited objectives are pursued the issue is not so much the teacher educators' intentions as the dynamics of the situation in which the student is placed. The critical questions therefore relate to the treatment of the student's experiential understanding rather than the formal structure of school experience. To what extent and in what ways are the students encouraged to make explicit and explore the views of children and teaching they themselves evolve and encounter while in schools? What is the relationship between such views and those 'ready-made' characterisations offered in theoretical parts of the course, as discussed above? And what value is accorded to the different views, definitions and perspectives - theoretical and experiential - which the student acquires or meets?

Hitherto, however, even in courses committed to Stage III above, the everyday, experiential perspective has probably counted for less than it might. There are, of course, problems in explicating and communicating these understandings. Being to a considerable extent private and idiosyncratic such knowledge is not readily expressed through the conceptual and linguistic structures currently on offer for public discourse about education. This may be a good example of the pervasive influence of behaviourist psychology on the initial training course as a whole. For although there is no good reason why the distrust of introspective methods should influence a part of the course which makes no claim to psychological status, the urge to assert the 'scientific' character of teaching and teacher training may result in what are perceived as scientific methodological criteria being applied across the board without regard to their appositeness. In terms of such criteria the perspectives of individual teachers could be deemed inadmissible. Moreover, difficulties in articulating and characterising such perspectives make for unflattering comparison with the apparent ease, sophistication and conceptual tidiness of academic modes of discourse. Everyday analysis, haltingly articulated, appears banal and brutish, a telling confirmation of the academic's disdain for 'mere' subjectivity, opinion and intuition.

In reality the reverse may well be the case: a complex, subtle conceptual may not readily amenable to expression in terms of the relatively crude public constructs offered by the existing, monopolistic modes of respectable educational theorising about such matters. Thus, for example, the general concept of 'typification' referred to at various points seems a potent one. What is less convincing is the claim that we can identify, in all their richness, diversity and paradox, exactly what a teacher's typifications and constructs are, using, for example, the relatively simplistic tool of repertory grid technique.

Where, then, lies the true banality: in the thinking and practice of teachers as such, or in the versions thereof offered by researchers and the procedures and models from which such versions are constructed? And what is being valued, depth of insight or sophistication of language? Fortunately, no simple answers to these questions are available: to provide them would be to compound the felony. But it can be suggested that the philosophical uncertainty surrounding the matter of how others' thoughts can be 'known' makes it inappropriate for teacher educators to accord such unequal status to 'academic' and 'everyday' versions of classroom reality. Take, for example, a course with a flexible 'workshop' concept of school experience, on which a student may be required, as now commonly happens, to come to 'understand' children's cognitive development by carrying out Piagetian tests in school. The rationale for this exercise is 'applying theory to practice', or. put another way, demonstrating the validity of the theory, confirming the Piagetian model. However, since in replicating the test the student will also have to replicate the circumstances, the result is predictable. What the replication does is simply to illustrate the hypothesis, not confirm it. Indeed, possibly the last thing the psychology tutor concerned may want is genuine testing of the model. We have then, two questionable assumptions endemic to teacher education and exemplified ever in State III 'progressive' models of school/course interaction, First, that the academic model of human behaviour is qualitatively superior to the everyday, less by virtue of its proven veracity than because of the context and manner in which it is generated and the language through which it is expressed. Second, that professional knowledge is acquired by making the idiosyncratically observed and experienced world 'fit' theoretical models of it; or, put another way, by theory verification rather than theory falsification.

Again, it seems to me, the impact of this kind of covert epistemology extends well beyond the immediate circumstances of initial training and will affect or support the everyday predilections of the serving teacher in respect of both his knowledge of the child and his view of the child's knowledge of the world. Despite the teaching profession's public scepticism about educational theory and research, its own characterisations of children and educational processes are heavily dependent upon their conceptual framework, but, crucially, simplified, as in the case of children's development and socio-cultural background which we have discussed, and as exemplified in the general tendency to conceive of empirical educational inquiry only in terms of quantification and proof.

Alternatives

To make use of schools not merely as a context for practising executive skills but as a prime means for developing the student's capacities to observe, understand and relate to children is a *sine qua non* of teacher education. It has to be asked, however, whether the opportunities are fully exploited. This is only partly, as we have seen, a procedural matter; what needs closer attention is the teacher educators' and course validators' view of what this 'understanding' might mean. At present, and certainly during the decade when today's primary teachers and heads trained, the interpretations, explanations and hypotheses of students and serving teachers have been under-valued and therefore insufficiently pursued and tested. And while a somewhat restricted canon of child-related theories has been, in comparison, over-exposed, it has been the exposure of obeisance, rather than critique. Some of the consequences, or correspondences, suggested by this restricted epistemology have been outlined in this chapter and exemplified more fully.

There seem to be a number of ways the situation can be improved, of varying degrees of radicalism:

(a) the focus for 'understanding' can be broadened;

(b) better use can be made of existing education disciplines;

(c) additional (academic) sources of insight can be explored;

(d) 'everyday' modes of understanding can be more fully exploited;

(e) different conceptions of professional theory for teaching can be applied.

Broadening the focus

In an obvious sense, by definition, students are the main concern in a course of initial training: the qualities, skills and knowledge which they are deemed to need are the course's raison d'etre. So in arguing that the course needs to focus more explicitly on the student and on the serving teacher I am arguing for a specific kind of attention with which this self-evident concern is not to be confused. Courses are premised on the importance of teachers' mastery of certain executive skills, their manifestation of particular personal qualities and their possession of certain kinds of knowledge. Pre-eminent among the latter is that academic knowledge about children which we have explored in this chapter, and which they may or may not make significant use of in practice. What, by and large, are neglected are the many layers or facets beyond these generalised propositions which combine to create the particular ways individual students and teachers actually view, or 'understand', the children they teach in particular classroom settings: teachers' actual and tacit, as opposed to preferred or espoused or idealised, knowledge of children, and the biographies which produce this knowledge: their subjective realities, as opposed to the quasi-objective ideas or the educational situation with which they are presented in training.

Merely to offer to the student a set of propositions from psychological/sociological theory or research—'this is the way children are, this is what they are like, this is the reality to which your decisions must be addressed'—is to ignore, or at least to fail to acknowledge sufficiently, two basic arguments concerning children in classrooms in which much of this book's discussion has been grounded. First, regardless of generalised principles of child development, motivation and so on, children are 'as they are' in classrooms, in part at least, because of the actions of the teacher; they respond, as in interaction all humans respond, to personality, to climate, to tacit or explicit signals, attitudes and expectations from a variety of sources, but chiefly, in the educational context, from the teacher. Second, though individual children are viewed differently by each of those with whom they interact, and their self-concept indeed in part evolves from a consciousness of these various perceptions, in the educational context the teacher's view of them is the most significant. It is the teacher who defines their abilities, their potential, their personality, their attainment and their attitudes, for the purposes of making curricular decisions, evaluations and predictions, and, as we have seen, in a way which is consistent with their ideology. Such is the nature of the educational process, and the classroom power relationship, especially where young children are concerned, that the central assumption in child-centredness, of the child's autonomy, is not only fallacious but dangerously so. It can never be the case that on the one hand we have the child, about whom there is pre-existing objective knowledge, and on the other the teacher, who simply has to acquire that knowledge. The teacher's knowledge of the child is subjective, it is created by the teacher, its character is therefore as strongly conditional on the way the teacher is as the way the child is.

The theme for initial training, which should complement 'understanding children' is 'understanding how teachers "understand" children'. And if it is indeed students understanding that we wish to promote rather than their capacity merely to parrot the prepositions and formulae of others, the source as well as the character of such 'understanding', on the basis of which students and teachers act, needs to be explored; this necessitate attention to the unique individual biographies of each students as well as to the more generalised analysis of the professional, historical and ideological situation of the particular groups of teachers offered. The outcome of this process should be to sensitise the student to the possibility of a much wider range of diagnoses and explanations. Traditionally, courses offer a limited range of answers to the teacher's question 'Why is this childlike this?'. The added dimension stems from the immediate preparedness to ask in addition: 'Why do I view the child in this way?' 'Is there an alternative diagnosis?' 'What is the connection between how I view the child and the sort of person I am? 'Between the child's behaviour and mine?' 'Which of the child's characteristics seem to be independent of the context within which the child and I operate?' 'What part does my personal history play in formulating my views and actions in the classroom?'

The phrases 'self-analysis', 'self-awareness' or 'self-criticism' only partly encompass what is required because conventionally they are affectivity-oriented, referring primarily to attitudes, motivation and emotional response: self-analysis in the present sense has to include, in addition, attention to one's personal and professional epistemology - the nature of one's knowledge about the children one teaches, its validity,its source, its limitations, its influence, and so on. The fact that introspective methods are unacceptable to some psychologists is worthy of debate in this context but is not grounds for rejecting the perspective I have defined. The course aims to train teachers, not professional psychologists, and if a perspective is helpful it should be included, methodological qualms notwithstanding.

Thus the scope of 'understanding children' in initial training needs to be broadened chiefly by taking in *teachers'* influence on both the children and their 'understanding' of them. Equally important, and more easily enunciated, is the need to allow existing perspectives on children offered by psychology and sociology to be supplemented by alternatives from within those disciplines. I tried to show how currently taught models of child development may feed the complacency surrounding primary class teaching while different psychological traditions might provide a basis for a keener appraisal. Clearly, given our discussion of the complementary relationship between ideology, professional theory and practical situation, the introduction of less comfortable psychologies and sociologies might be resisted, but perhaps we can begin to accept that our comfort may well be secured at the expense of the quality of the child's education.

This shift has already begun in the sociology of education: the sociology of knowledge and of classrooms has provided the needed counterbalance to the family/home educability preoccupations of the 1950s and 1060s. We now need a 'new' psychology of education which more fairly represents the richness of mainstream psychology.

The newer perspectives offer both alternative focuses and tools for analysis. Centre-stage are not only classroom processes and the interactions of teachers and children which feature in 'objective' study in the Flanders tradition, but also the meanings which the teachers and children themselves assign to those processes. The underlying assumption here is that human actions can be properly understood only if one uncovers these meanings, since 'action is forged by the actor out of what he perceives, interprets and judges... The "objective" approach holds the danger of the observer substituting his view of the field of action for the view held by the actor,.

Equally important, we are presented with an alternative view of the self which might prompt us to look as closely at the child now, in the classroom, as at supposedly fixed and unalterable attributes like intelligence, personality and home background:

All human beings are possessed of a self ...they are reflexive or self-interacting.. We think about what we are doing, and what goes on inside our heads is a crucial element in how we act. The self is...not a fixed structure, frozen by our toilet training or early conditioning, but rather a dynamic, changing process.

This basic perspective influences, to varying degrees and in different ways, most members of the family of the 'new' sociology of education which has emerged since the early 1970s, some of which I have either referred to directly in this and earlier chapters or have allowed to penetrate, albeit loosely, my own analysis. What divides the family is the extent to which action can be studied and interpreted exclusively in terms factors' meanings. Strictly applied, *social phenomenology* examines events in their own terms and resists explanations in terms of wider social and economic forces. Sharp and Green's study of a 'progressive' primary school found this an unacceptably purist paradigm and injected a *Marxist* perspective so as to show how primary schooling both reflects and reinforces prevailing societal structures and ideologies. More determinist still, the notion of schooling in general, and curriculum in particular, as mechanisms of social control and cultural reproduction, is prominently represented in the work of Young and in the collection of papers edited for the Open University by Dale, Esland and MacDonald. Moving back towards phenomenology, but representing in terms of historical origin a parallel rather than a related movement, and not asserting actors' total independence from societal structures and forces, *symbolic interactionism* gives prominence to actors' meanings but focuses especially upon the process whereby these are arrived at, often through 'negotiation'. Thus, in studying classrooms it becomes important to understand pupils' as well as teachers' definitions of the situation, and the extent to which the latter are not autonomous but are influenced by the former; at the same time the power differential in classrooms makes the impact of teachers' meanings on children and classroom life considerable. This perspective prominently informs the classic and comprehensive exploration of school interaction by Hargreaves and specific studies of primary classrooms like that of Berlak et al. The study of infants' classrooms by King, to which I have made frequent reference, is eclectic: it is critical of phenomenological, interactionist and Marxist perspectives yet is also influenced by them. It belongs to the 'family' in so far as it is grounded in close and sustained observation which is interpreted by reference to actors' perceptions and explanations rather than observer preconceptions. At the same place time it places these in broader frameworks of ideology and social structure.

These developments are recent: empirical study of primary classrooms, of whatever methodological complexion, is still relatively thin. Nevertheless, in terms of what by this book''s analysis seems to be needed—far greater attention to how teachers 'understood' children and teaching —the growth points are now significant, diverse and rich.

Making better use of 'the disciplines'

The last point notwithstanding, we also need to ask whether the monopoly by psychology and sociology of insights into children and classrooms is to be desired or supported. The other two disciplines in the educational studies pantheon are philosophy and history. Philosophy of education - whether so defined or used thematically in an integrated course—tends to concern itself with broad non-contextualised questions about aims, the nature of knowledge, the justification for particular educational concepts and activities, the ethics of reward and punishment. Frequently it is conceived as a tool of encouraging a sharper, more reflexive and considered mode of analysis than the easy, instant judgement, as a basis for critique of teachers' and students' 'commonsense' statements. This is undoubtedly necessary, but it is also the case that by such means, intentionally or unwittingly, is the status of academic thought preserved, for philosophical analysis ought equally to be applied to the statements, judgement and explanations offered by psychology and sociology of education: conceptual analysis should have no boundaries. Especially, a concern with epistemology ought not to start and finish with the school curriculum, but should encompass the knowledge and truth claims of the teacher training curriculum as well, the ways of making sense of and understanding children, teaching and learning which the initial training course expects the student to internalise and subsequently 'apply' in the classroom. In other words, 'ways of knowing' about educational processes should be subjected to the same level of scrutiny as are the ways of knowing which constitute the school curriculum out there in the school. To fail to do this is to miss an opportunity to give the student a working understandingof epistemological issues;

and it could be construed as hypothetical to subject to critique the school curriculum but not that of teacher education.

A similar argument applies in the case of history of education. We saw that how usefully a historical awareness of the institutional and ideational background of primary education both illuminates and provides a basis for critique of present-day ideas and practices, particularly in respect of the ways of the child is viewed and the curriculum defined in the context of the class-teacher system. We also saw how primary professional discourse with its 'cocoon' imaginary and polarising of the child and society, seems resistant to a sense of the interplay of historical events, cultural values and educational ideals. Conventionally, history of education courses have done little to remedy this. Courses in 'the educational system of England and Wales' can still be as normative, functionalist, systemic and superficial as they were in the years following the NcNair Report: resumes of the clauses of education acts and the recommendations of major reports, but rarely interpretations or explanation beyond a sort of sub 'O' level 'seven causes of the Boer War' variety, and certainly little real delving into the pedagogy and curriculum experienced by previous generations of children and the justifications offered by teachers and others in support of these. 'Why do we view children like this?' 'Why do we define their educational needs in this way?': these are questions as much historical as psychological, and the desire to ask them is surely a prerequisite for any teacher in a complex, changing, pluralist society.

Teaching is constituted of ideas as well as action; indeed it is the putting into operation of ideas. These need to be explicated, critically explored and, to be properly understood, need to be culturally and historically located.

Beyond 'the disciplines'

Of course academic monopolies are not fortuitous: the one under discussion reflects aspirations to make teaching a 'science' grounded in a set of empirically derived principles and so to demonstrate the 'expert knowledge' basis of the teacher's professional claim. However, we might try asking afresh, with no preconditions, the open question: 'What is the best way to develop the young adult's capacity to understand other human beings, especially pre-adolescent children?'in pursuit of an answer we might attempt to catalogue those ways which humans have learned to understand each other and themselves. On the one hand, and prominently, there is the pervasiveness and potential of insight grounded in individual and collective experience. I return to this below, but if, meanwhile, we concentrate more on academic or public modes of personal and inter-personal exploration, we have to acknowledge, as I argued earlier, that the field can encompass, at least, literature, art, music, drama and religion as well as the social sciences; and that even the latter can extend much further than teacher education has allowed - for example in include social anthropology and social psychology. The modes of inquiry we actually make available to the student are from one small spectrum of human knowledge, and, as it happens, they are from one of the newest and - to workers in the physical sciences and the arts alike - one of the most suspect in terms of its claims to represent humans as they are.

Putting into operation such extended concepts of 'understanding children and teachers' is not necessarily easy, but the issue needs to be faced. As presently conceived, teacher education courses place arbitrary and unnecessary restrictions on this aspect of the student's development. In the first instance courses could be released from that 'compartmentalisation of function' I referred to earlier and each component could be scrutinised as to its potential for generation insight and skill useful to the intending primary teacher, regardless academics' claims or territorial anxieties. The most basic reappraisal would concern the academic/professional distinction, and, as a consequence, the common ground between subject studies and education theory as regards each's capacity both to generate professional insight and to met 'personally educative' functions might be disconcerting.

Rehabilitating the 'everyday'

However, the most substantial and necessary shift in this context is towards the exploration and use in initial training of non-academic, everyday, subjective professional knowledge. The arguments seem inescapable: such knowledge is pervasive, inevitable and influential in everyday practice and therefore requires exploration; it is effective in that it is the basis for teaching of a high quality and therefore may encapsulate ideas worthy of emulation; it is also, conversely, the basis for weak teaching and therefore its limitations as well as its strengths need to be exposed. Where, as in this context, the everyday knowledge in question concerns children, it taps, or may tap, insights stemming from one of the most fundamental of human relationships: it cannot simply be disregarded on the grounds of arbitrary stimulative definitions of what constitutes 'science' and 'objectivity'.

This is not an argument for rejecting academic inquiry, or for a revival of apprenticeship approaches to teacher education. Rather, the case is made for recognising the strengths and limitations of any mode of understanding pursued in overmuch isolation - particular disciplines, academic study in general, personal, experientially grounded everyday knowledge - and for acknowledging the advantage of using these in combination and juxtaposition, particularly in pursuit of that understanding of ourselves and others which educationists seem happily prepared to lay claim to, despite the fact that the rest of humanity has found it rather more elusive.

Such eclecticism as is argued here would be conditional upon courses sensitising students to the epostemological problems raised. It is not adequate to 'raid the disciplines', or rather to 'raid' all available and potentially productive sources of insight, without also understanding the nature of the truth claim each makes and the limitations thereof. Traditionally courses have tended to treat academic sources as given the experiential sources as suspect or unacceptable: all are problematic, though in different ways.

Reconceptualising professional theory

It will be apparent by now that, in combination, the ideas above require not minor adjustment to the content and pedagogy of initial training courses, but a more fundamental shift. The operational question is 'What kind of professional theory does the intending primary class teacher need in order to understand and relate successfully to and provide valid educational experiences for young children?'

This present chapter has tried to show how the answer to this question involves matters of epistemology as well as content; the related questions are: 'To what extent is teaching a science?' 'Is the attempt so to dignify it appropriate?' 'Exactly what kind of an activity *is* teaching?'

These matters do not concern the particular focus of the present chapter alone, and are therefore discussed after the consideration of the training for the curricular requirements of class teaching.

5 School-based Curriculum Development in Theory and Practice

'School-based curriculum development' is a clumsy term, used to refer to activities which, because they take place in the unique contexts of individual schools, are necessarily diverse. This chapter attempts to place some structure on the idea of school-based curriculum development by linking material from four relevant areas. First, *theoretical concepts* are outlined; second, these concepts are qualified by reference to the *practice* of curriculum development in primary schools; third, *contextual factors* influencing the nature of such development are examined; and finally, the *values* underlying school-based curriculum development in primary schools are briefly elaborated.

Concepts of school-based curriculum development

One of the problems faced by anyone attempting to understand school-based curriculum development as an idea is that it is used very much as a catch-all concept. For example, as illustrated by Mitson, it means something as substantial as groups of secondary school pupils, together with appropriate staff training and resources development; or it may be small-scale revision of a language programme in a primary school, such that described by Timms and Lees.

The DES has stressed the significance of school-based approach, but two writers in particular have helped to sharpen the formulation of ideas about them. Eggleston's introduction to six case studies provides a useful starting-point:

Although it is unclear whether Eggleston was describing school-based curriculum development or prescribing a particular way of doing it, four features of his definition are worth picking out:

1. It is *particularistic*: The curriculum-development activity is focused upon the diagnosed, or perceived, needs of the specific school or part of it.
2. It is *process-oriented*: In the terms of 'strategies for the curriculum' intended, the process by which these are developed in important in itself.
3. It is *participatory*: The appropriate style for developing the curriculum is cooperative, that is, staff working together to produce plans for change.
4. It is *preliminary*: The curriculum developed is to be seen an experimental, in the sense that it is open to evaluation and appraisal after its implementation.

One of the interesting things about this definition is the stress, not on the curriculum as such, but on the *roles* that teachers have to play in the process of its development, and the attitudes that are required to underpin it.

This characteristic is also central to the analysis offered by another writer, Skilbeck. He identified three models of school-based curriculum development—the *rational-deductive*, the *rational-interactive* and the *intuitive*—and located them within differing politico-educational frameworks. The first operates in centrally directed educational systems, where the task of the school is to 'interpret central directives' and the role of the teacher is as a mere functionary in a bureaucratised educational service. The second emerges in mixed systems, such as those in England and Wales, which stress the active role of teachers in adapting the curriculum at school level within rather broad general outlines of national policy. Teachers working within this kind of framework have a more complex role than in the rational-deductive model and have more demands made upon them; they 'have to act as course assessors, to help construct syllabuses, to select learning materials and to devise learning systems'. The third model stresses the individual teacher's decision-making and creativity, and leads to great diversity between teachers between schools, and to inconsistency between 'normal policy and individual school programmes'.

Although school-based curriculum development may share elements from all three, the rational-interactive model represents the style and values most appropriate to contemporary English schools, especially because of the stress put upon the range of roles expected of teachers, and the assumption that teachers have to negotiate the fine details of their roles by working in partnership with each other. Thus in this formulation also, school-based curriculum development is as much about changing roles and relationships among a school staff as it is about changing schemes of work or methods of teaching and learning.

A second paper by Skilbeck offered a substantial analysis of the concept, rationale and aims of school-based curriculum development, and suggested a model for school use, with a commentary on the difficulties in implementing it. He identified a number of characteristics, including the idea of the curriculum as a set of:

> Experiences of value developed by the teacher and learner together from a close and sympathetic appraisal of the learner's needs and characteristics as a learner.

But, although Skilbeck identified the need for freedom for the teachers to define relevant learning experiences, he also noted the requirement for appropriate support systems, including national or regional curricular guidelines. This is an important point, not least t counteract the danger of a simplistic polarising of 'school-based' and 'non-school-based' approaches to curriculum development. A major goal of school-based curriculum development in Skilbeck's terms is the continuous adaption by teachers of externally defined curricula into forms of educative experiences unique to the teacher and learner.

We need a system for curriculum development that combines the advantages of national policy making, national centres for the production of materials and for research and development, with the flexibility, adaptability, and professionally satisfying features of local initiatives and creativity.

Thus school-based curriculum development is predicated upon the concept, admittedly idealised, of teachers who creatively reconstruct the curriculum within a recognised framework of local and national expectations; it is not predicted upon passive acceptance of external definitions of the curriculum, or the myth of the 'autonomous' school, existing independently of its political and economic context. Given the political development, outlined, of a national framework for the curriculum, the relevance of Skilbeck's model for teachers in England and Wales has increased considerably.

Skilbeck's analysis enables us to add two further characteristics of school-based curriculum development to the four identified earlier. These concern the relationship between the school's curriculum and national or local guidelines, and the view taken of the role of the teacher. We can summarise these by saying that school-based curriculum development is:

1. *Framework adaptive.* Despite its particularistic focus, it need not run counter to national or

local curriculum guidelines, but may on the contrary ride on them, if staff adapt them to suit their specific situation.

2. *Role extensive* Issues acceptance by teachers of a wider role than that restricted to classroom performance and it consequently assumes change, or flexibility, in their existing roles.

The teacher as educationalist

The teacher role in curriculum development, discussed in the theoretical positions encapsulated above, is to do with what Keddie called the 'teacher-as-educationist' context. In her study of a secondary school teachers, Keddie noted two different aspects of their activities: their role beliefs and practices in the context of their classrooms when instructing pupils; and their beliefs and practices elaborated in extra-classroom situations, when discussing educational ideas and principles with colleagues, and with outsiders such as advisors and parents. Keddie's somewhat jaundiced view of the disparity of beliefs between the two contexts need not concern us here, but the distinction itself is very fruitful for analysing teachers' roles in school-based curriculum development. For most of their time, teachers in the Warwick inquiry were, as *curriculum developers*, operating in the educationalist context, that is to say in situations where they were required to discuss educational policies and practices with their colleagues and other adults. This is a fairly novel role for teachers in primary schools, where traditionally it has been reserved for the headteacher, if anyone. More commonly it has been allocated to the local-authority advisers or other educationists in courses located, and often focused, far from the contexts of the schools themselves.

Eggleston and Skilbeck have provided a frame within which a fairly well-defined picture of school-based curriculum development can be held. It is dominated by *process*—by teachers collaborating in working groups as professionals to interpret general curricular assumptions into a specific curriculum practice suitable for their particular context. This process requires teachers to develop a role for themselves as educationalists in the sense that they will have to familiarise themselves with national and local curriculum documents, justify and articulate curricular objectives, implement and sustain innovation, and evaluate and account for it. Thus the distinctive arena for school-based curriculum development is the staffroom rather than the classroom, and the distinctive discourse is concerned not only with the surface details of curriculum practice, but also with the assumptions underlying it.

Curriculum development in practice: gradualism and specialism

The theoretical analyses discussed above are necessarily generalised, and need to be qualified somewhat in the light of the practice in the Warwick inquiry schools. Brief outlines of the programmes have already been provided, which suggest two characteristics that are perhaps distinctive to primary school curriculum development. They can be considered under two headings, namely *gradualism* and *specialism*. To dichotomise rather too simply, gradualism qualifies the idea of 'development', while specialism qualifies the idea of 'curriculum'.

Gradualism

By gradualism I means three related features of the notion of 'development which stress the limited expectations that may be held for it. These three limitations may be thought of as the *problematic*, the *unpredictable* and the *incremental* qualities of curriculum development in primary schools.

The problematic nature of curriculum development derives from the fact that there is a conceptual difference between development and change. The latter is neutral and implies merely that practice has altered, not that it has been improved. 'Development', 'renewal' and probably 'innovation' imply not merely change, but change for the better. What counts as a change for the better in education is problematic. An analogy with the practice of medicine may he helpful. If a doctor diagnoses, say, constipation in a patient and prescribes a change of diet as a remedy, there is not much professional or lay disagreement about what would constitute a change for the better in the patient's condition. Not being constipated is generally regarded as an improvement on being so. But the school curriculum is a more difficult area for diagnosis, with less sure a basis for agreement about what constitutes improvement. A curriculum where there has been, so to speak, little movement for a number of years is not necessarily in a worse condition than one in which there has been a great deal of it.

One of the points that follows from this is that, although the term 'curriculum development' is widely used throughout the literature and in this book, in practice it cannot be shown in advance, and often it is not known even in retrospect, whether changes are actually developments. At best it is commonly a matter of belief, intuition and professional judgement of those involve. Indeed, to return to Eggleston's emphasis on the *process* of development, it was quite striking to note how frequently the teachers in the Warwick inquiry reported that the major benefit, for them, of school-based development activities had been the experience of being involved in the process rather than, or in addition to, any changes in actual curriculum practice. It was as though they were hedging their bets on the curricular outcome of the initiatives.

Second, there is *lack of predictability* in outcome. Given the experimental approach characterised by Eggleston as 'discussion, planning, trial and evaluation', there is the built-in risk that the evaluation might show no tangible development in the desired direction. This seems to have been the case in the Oxfordshire primary school reported in a case study for the Open University prepared by Clift. He reported a self-evaluation exercise by the school staff, lasting over a year, and involving at least seven in-school staff meetings, to prepare a review of the school's policy, provision and practices across a range of activities, including the curriculum. It appears to have been characterised by serious, professional involvement by the staff, and to have been efficiently and yet flexibly organised. It covered, among many other matters, problems or curricular aims and how they should be described, curricular practice, including the grouping of pupils and catering for individual differences, and the provision of curricular guidelines, and was carried out by effective teacher collaboration. The case study author reported in the postscript that the changes that followed this activity were:

(a) a new duplicator;

(b) a loss of a member of staff without replacement;

(c) a new staff toilet.

It is perhaps very much to be hoped that, for these teachers, the process of their endeavours was valued at least as highly as products. But it does illustrate in an extreme way the uncertainty of school-based development—its almost chancy nature and the unpredictability of its outcomes. As Shipman writing about larger-scale curriculum development activities.

A third characteristic of the notion of development in the curriculum in *incrementalism*: that what is involved is not a fundamental change, but an extension of existing practices. The foundations of the school's curriculum are not being dug up and re-laid: the structure of the curriculum is being renovated a little, that is all. This kind of development cannot promise or deliver a dramatically different curriculum. It is not designed to do that, nor is it resourced adequately for it. The kind of sweeping changes in curricular aims and practices currently being promoted for the 14-19 years-olds, for example, could not easily be developed in the school-based mode precisely because they are predicted upon external intervention fundamentally to redefine curricular aims at least in the innovation period. School-based curriculum development is a more modestly conceived activity, designed to build upon existing mainstream curricular practice, and predicated upon the assumption of a curricular framework about which there is already consensus, or which can be taken for granted. It is incremental, not radical, change in the curriculum, with slow, small-scale, granted. It is incremental, not radical, change in the curriculum, with slow, small-scale, almost routine, benefits, accruing over time from a school staff gradually building upon its collective strengths and, where possible, remedying weaknesses. There should be little of the heady rhetoric associated with large-scale national projects of the 1960s and early 1970s, not just because such rhetoric tends to lack credibility in the routine of school life, but because school-based approaches are designed to improve the normal curriculum, not graft abnormal practices on to it.

Discussions with teachers in the Warwick inquiry illustrated the incremental quality in an interesting way, showing the mundane and highly pragmatic nature of what was involved. In School 1, a staff group met to review their curricular policy in social studies, and attempted to revise an existing scheme by constructing it around some basic concepts and skills, drawn partly from some Schools Council curriculum materials and partly from their experience with the previous scheme. No grand claims were made, or were felt necessary to be made, about either the changes that might follow or the process itself.

Many frameworks were tried in private and rejected; it was felt important to demonstrate that the content..could be organized-conceptually. To test this we developed a matrix, setting four broad conceptual areas of Environmental Studies across four conceptual themes from 'Home and Family'. When we did this, we simply jotted down in the matrix what we thought would work, given that had worked before, and the overall conceptual scheme we were developing. And then we met and locked at what we'd written down and tried to sort it our from there.

What strikes one about these statements is their very ordinates, their tentativeness and the absence of extravagance is what is being claimed. They are the voices of routine improvement not radical, or even substantial, change, expressing the gradual, incremental quality of school-based curriculum development at primary-school level. They embody the view of HMI that:

A slow but steady build up from the points of strength of individual teachers is probably the only way forward.

Specialism

Specialism refers to the exploitation of expertise in a subject or, more accurately, in a curriculum area. This exploitation took a variety of forms in practice but three can be distinguished: specialist teaching, subject teaching and subject diffusion.

Specialist teaching

This occurred in two cases, with teachers used to teach a number of classes and having no class responsibility themselves. The two cases provide ambivalent evidence, limited though it is, for the idea of specialist teaching as a basis for in-school development. Both teachers taught their subject to all the older children in the school, but non the less needed to influence the quality of work with the younger children, who were taught by class teachers. They exercised responsibility for raising the quality of work done throughout the school, though they also acknowledged a reduced impact upon the younger classes. They appear to have experienced little of the conflict and strain that other postholders felt, as reported. This was probably because teaching one subject and not having class responsibilities dramatically reduced the range of the other demands made upon specialists.

On the other hand, as suggests, the two teachers used as specialists tended to have involved their colleagues less in the process of curriculum development than did other postholders. Furthermore, the specialist teachers did not involve colleagues in evaluation of their programmes. This suggests, accepting that these are two cases only, that specialist teaching, whatever its merits in classroom practice of the specialist, may, in terms of initiatives of a school-wide kind, tend to produce leadership of a more isolated, less collective style than would otherwise be the case.

Subject teaching

This occurred when teachers with specialist subject knowledge taught one or two other classes on a regular basis, while retaining a generalist class-teaching role with their own class. This occurred in two cases. A related version of subject teaching was when a teacher irregularly, and for limited specific purposes, taught alongside colleagues, or swapped classes, in order to teach a specialist topic or skill or to demonstrate a skill and show the quality of work that could be expected. This happened in three other cases.

Subject diffusion

This occurred in all the programmes, when teachers with expertise were consulted by others who needed advice, or when they took a lead in curriculum planning and review groups. It was the main mechanism for spreading specialist knowledge from the post-holder to the other staff. It was what the Inspectorate meant when they talked of postholders' having an 'influence' on the work throughout a primary school. With organisational arrangements reflecting the class-teacher principle, even where some subject teaching occurred, this diffusion model was the dominant style of in-school development.

One of the heads explained the approach in the following terms:

We has specialist teaching here some years ago, and given our staffing we could still use it much more than we do. But we've more or less abandoned it, except for French and our Remedial Specialist...There are two reasons. The main one is that the children here need a lot of structure and the class teacher provides that best of all...So the second reason follows once you've decided that. It is to *use* teachers who were specialists to lead curriculum review groups, and we've been doing that here for the last couple of years now...it doesn't always come off, but it's staff development as well as curriculum development.

The stress on the use of teacher specialism in the curriculum development programmes is largely explicable in terms of the political analysis. All the programmes, except for cases B and J, were focused on issues raised in the Primary Survey, which stressed the need to provide for greater progression and continuity, to cater for able children, to fill the gap in science, to extend advanced reading skills, and so on. Although it may not be a permanent characteristic of primary school curriculum development, it probably provides quite strong evidence of the impact of the survey, an impact followed up in two later surveys by HMI in which 'specialisation' and its contribution to curriculum development in first and middle schools were further examined.

The context of school-based curriculum development

There is an ecology of curriculum development. Just as certain kinds of plant and animal life flourish in favourable conditions of soil, light, temperature and the balance of relationships in their overall environment, so the context of primary schools inhibits or encourages the growth of the kind of curriculum development discussed above. Factors in this context can be considered as *external* to the school or *internal* to it, although the distinction is not clear cut. External factors are those derived from the educational system itself, from its administration, finance, demography and from teacher career opportunities. Internal factors include the role relationships of teachers and the ways in which authority is exercised by the headteacher.

External influences

Staffing and resource allocations

The objective raw indices of PTRs in primary schools have shown a progressive small improvement over the past decade, with the national primary mean PTR moving from 25.0:1 in 1973 to 21.8:1 in 1983. The rate has slowed down in the last three years, but the trend is still towards improvement. Moreover, the proportion of classes with over 30 pupils has also reduced, according to data released by Joseph. Both kinds of 'improvements' are partly created by falling rolls, which require some relatively small classes to be tolerated. There is considerable evidence that small improvements in PTR and/or class size are not associated with raised standards of attainment, and it is probable that the marginal changes in PTR and class size do not, of themselves, positively or adversely affect a school's potential for curriculum renewal.

In a period of contraction, the range of skills and expertise within a staff group and the way they are deployed may be a more critical matter for curriculum development than PTR. The contraction in the school population may affect the potential of an individual school in two ways. It may push a school into competition—however unwillingly—for pupil numbers, or rather for parental esteem, with a neighbouring school with which it would previously have been seeking co-operation. In this context curriculum innovation which might be considered risky, is unlikely. More important, however, overall staff expertise may be affected, because the impact of falling rolls will lead to loss of flexibility in the ways that staff can be used, and sometimes to arbitrary loss of specialism. Even if staffing is reduced in line with pupil numbers, a school's ability to deploy teachers in ways that can effectively exploit their skills and expertise will become limited and, most crucially perhaps, the opportunities to free teachers for necessary curriculum development activities in school time will be lost.

It is for this reason that some local authorities have developed what they refer to as 'curriculum-led' staffing policies. Although there is a suspicion that such policies could be used primarily to decide that small schools are not viable, an interesting consequence of them is that the local authority has to make clear what its conception of an adequate primary school curriculum is, for curriculum-led staffing policies in effect move from a ratio as an index of staffing policy which emphasised.

The minimum number of classes that each type of primary school ought to be able to form if a satisfactory curriculum is to be available to pupils.

It went further towards defining the curriculum by which is staffing policy should be led:

If an adequate middle school curriculum is to be provided ... then the staffing must provide- in addition to the requisite number of class teachers - some who are capable of specialising in science, craft, foreign language and music.

Thus, in theory at least, staffing allocations, and curriculum-led staffing policies, can be seen as supporting school-based curriculum development. Precisely because, having broadly defined the curriculum provision thought to be appropriate, they highlight the need to identify, develop and exploit staff expertise in order to maintain and renew the local authority, conception of the primary school curriculum. This still obtains as a principle, even where teacher-redeployment strategies adopt criteria other than curricular specialism. At the present time it is unclear whether decisions about which teachers should be redeployed are based on curricular demands, degree of seniority or local political pragmatism; probably all three are involved to differing degrees. There is no logical reason why redeployment of staff should in itself reduce curriculum development possibilities, assuming that the nettle of curriculum-led staffing priorities can be grasped. Put at its most basic this would mean that a teacher with essential specialist curricular expertise would not be redeployed simply because he or she might be the youngest, or the most vulnerable, or the least likely to cause a fuss, or a part-timer. Equally, it might mean that a teacher with expertise in a shortage area might work in two schools rather than, as is normal, only one,

In the recent past the real value of capitation resources allocated to schools has fallen quite substantially, and in some local authorities the reductions were regarded by HMI as endangering educational standards. Although it is a truism to say that such reduction adversely affect the potential of a school staff to improve their curricular provision, the effects will vary greatly according to the nature of the particular curriculum development programme. There is a great difference in impact of resource expenditure upon a programme requiring for its introduction in a school the purchase of new sets of materials and equipment and one requiring different applications of existing materials and approaches. It has been argued earlier that school-based approaches in primary schools tended to be developments of existing practices, and resource reductions may go some way towards explaining that feature. If so, it suggests that such reductions will influence the nature of school-based development, rather than stifle its growth entirely.

Teachers' perceptions of contraction

The objective experience of contraction may not necessarily be the most powerful constraint upon development; the ways in which such contraction is perceived subjectively by teachers may be a far more important determinant. Put crudely, curriculum development depends much more upon the ability of a staff to harness its collective energy and enthusiasm than upon marginal reductions in staffing, or even real reductions in resources. It is upon teacher morale that the progress of innovation hangs, and morale itself has been damaged by contraction. In part, the impact of contraction has been cumulatively routine, with teachers coming in each morning to uncleaned rooms, dusty desks and other evidence of reduced expenditure, which has nothing directly to do with the curriculum, but which effectively eats away at teacher enthusiasm. But the dramatic impact is upon the teachers' perceptions of reduced career and promotion opportunities, which are real enough and may help to discourage innovation amongst career-minded teachers.

This is, however, very much a two-edged sword. Under an expanding system, teachers were sucked up into senior posts by a kind of capillary action and, having obtained their promotion, would demonstrate their merit afterwards. They would be given their special-responsibility allowances and then earn them. In a contracting system such promotion as there is will have to be earned in advance. As a local-authority adviser put it:

> Previously we promoted Mrs X in order that she would develop science in a school; now we may be able to reward her *if* he has developed it. And this has to apply to Scale 1 teachers as well - they will have to learn to lead other teachers in an area of the curriculum before they get a responsibility post.

Of course the degree of certainty of promotion differed in the two situations. However, the point about shrinking career opportunities is that they too will be perceived differently; some teachers will doubtless be confirmed in their view that there is no point to curriculum development if it is not certain to be rewarded, whilst for others it will at least be a surrogate for, and at best a precursor to, promotion. It would be unrealistic to ignore such a factor in examining the context of primary school curriculum development, and it may be for that reason that a number of recent commentaries have, included the notion that it should help to raise morale and channel the professional energies of teachers who would previously have been promoted more easily.

There is, however, a small irony in the situation. Whatever the general disadvantages of reduced promotion opportunities, from the point of vies of school-based development there is one advantage. For development of this kind to be originated, implemented and above all maintained requires, a relatively permanent, or at least stable, staff group. Frequent and widespread teacher mobility is not conducive to school-based approaches to curriculum development.

Thus the impact of the external factors, even in a contracting system, upon a school's ability to develop its curriculum is not overwhelmingly and inevitably adverse. Perhaps the most optimistic element is that primary pupil rolls are expected to stabilise in the mid-1980s and arbitrary loss of specialist skills within a staff group will occur less often. A further issue in the next decade, currently being canvassed in some local authorities and nationally, is the idea that INSET could become part of the contractual obligation of teachers. If this were to be successfully negotiated it would give considerable impetus to school-based curriculum development, especially if, as is also being considered, it is allied to earmarked resources and a re-aligned career structure for teachers.

Internal influences

Much of the discussion in the literature about school-based curriculum development is implicitly about secondary schools, so that internal issues raised are problems of relationships between subject departments, of development 'across the curriculum' and of managing large institutions.

For primary schools the internal factors pressing upon change are different. Two have been clearly identified; *zones of authority and devolution of curricular decision making.*

Zones of authority ; the classroom and the school

'Zones of authority' were a focus of a study of primary schools by Taylor, Reid, Holley and Exon, who reported and analysed the views of primary school teachers on the 'operational' curriculum. i.e. the curriculum in practice in a school. They identified two separate zones of authority; the classroom and the school. In terms of perceived influence, the classroom was by far the stronger zone and, if generalisable, their findings suggest clear obstacles to the development of school-wide policies on the curriculum, for if teachers see their classrooms as the major arena for their control over the curriculum, any attempt to develop it from a different basis by locating the development in the arena of the whole school is likely to start from a position of relative weakness. Individual teachers may opt out, regard it as interference, or simply alter any school-wide policy in the privacy of their own classrooms, legitimising their behaviour by invoking autonomy. The issue is peculiarly strong in primary schools, which are hierarchically ungraded, and where a teacher leading a curriculum development activity is in a position of equality with his or her colleagues, even if he or she has superior expertise in a particular field. The contrast between the formal and perceived power position of the secondary school head of department. seen as senior and officially recognised as such, and that of the primary school scale postholder is very great.

Devolution of decision-making and the authority of the head

Recognised authority, in respect of the primary school curriculum, is nearly always perceived as residing in the office of headteacher. There is a legal basis for this, but in an age when a broad liberal curriculum in mathematics, English, Science, art, music, craft, physical education and social and moral understanding is expected to be offered to all children, the notion of the headteacher as an authority in all these fields is no longer credible, if it ever was. There is therefore a mismatch between authority and responsibility for the curriculum in primary schools, with teachers who are responsible for developing aspects of the curriculum in which they are the 'expert' having little in the way of formal authority ascribed to them, and the headteachers, who have the authority, lacking the expertise. Lack of formal status is compounded for postholders by lack of informal recognition from their colleagues, according to HMI, who found few primary schools in which the postholders had a school-wide influence in their subject.

It is disappointing to find that the great majority of teachers with posts of special responsibility have little influence at present on the work of other teachers.

There are some practical implications of this comment for the primary school post-holder's workload, but the major issue concerns the attitudes of primary school staff toward curricular authority. Some shift towards a kind of collaborative decision-making about curriculum matters has been proposed by a number of commentators on primary schools, including Coulson and Razzell, although the latter appears, as Harling shows, to understate the obstacles to such an approach being adopted generally. The problem may not be so much the attitudes of headteachers as those of other teachers. When headteachers delegated responsibility and authority to their deputies, according to Coulson and Cox, the problem was that other teachers did not accept the transfer of authority as legitimate.

This brief review of the internal factors has been deliberately uncritical of them in order to report in summery form the prevailing view of the internal culture of primary schools. This internal culture is seen as structuring both teacher relationships in primary schools and teacher perceptions of curricular authority in classrooms and schools so as to provide a major constraint on postholder-led curriculum initiatives development. A critical re-analysis of the relevant studies is provided which suggests that in some respects teacher relationships and teacher attitudes, although still a problem, are beginning to change.

However, the view that attitudes and teacher relationships are critical to the success of school-based curriculum development, and probably more critical than the external resource and policy factors, was supported not simply by studies of

English primary schools, but also by a report in which an international perspective on the school context was provided. The findings of this report are discussed below.

OECD's the creativity of the school'

The cross-national study on the 'creativity' of schools carried out for OECD defined creativity much as school-based curriculum development has been defined in this chapter:

> A school's creativity is an awareness within the school of the problems it faces, a capacity to devise and adopt solutions whether initiated from outside or generated internally, and a willingness to evaluate their effectiveness.

A major interest of the study was the factors influencing school creativity, and two of these, which reflect the external/internal dichotomy above, were:

(a) administrative relationships between the school and outside institutions;

(b) organisation and relationships within the school.

The report offered three findings of particular relevance. It commented first on staffing/resources, second on school relationships, and third on teacher autonomy.

The problems of stimulating innovation in systems where promotion was impossible or difficult were examined in the report. It raised doubts on economic grounds about the efficiency of substantially and contractually reducing teaching duties so that curriculum innovation could be sustained, although it accepted the usefulness of limited reduction for a particular specified purpose; Perhaps most interestingly it doubted the utility of limited reductions in class size as a way of enhancing the creativity of the school. It concluded:

> Rather than seeking a general, across-the-board increase in teaching resources, schools should be encouraged selectively to redeploy existing resources to support creative innovation and in particular to provide incentives to key teachers to initiate or implement desirable changes.

Second, the report looked at the relationship between creativity and the internal organisation of the school. It identified four types of school organisation: authoritarian / bureaucratic, consultative, collegial, and full participatory. The collegial type is an organisation where decision-making is in the hands of the professional teaching staff, and the head acts as an executive. In consultative organisations, the power of decision-making remains with the head, but power is delegated and procedures for consulting teachers, students and parents are set up. These two organisational types were less likely to inhibit effective creativity than the other two.

The explanation for the greater effectiveness of these types is probably connected with the report's view that focusing upon the individual teacher was not the best way to induce change:

the individual teacher working alone in his classroom is an inappropriate unit. Rather, the small group of teachers with their group of students should be the basic unit of organisation. This is necessary both for interpersonal stimulation and essential mutual support. Such groups, which need not be stable over a long period, would be untied by a common task but could be organised in many different ways.

Of particular interest is the study's commentary on the problems associated with professional development in a collegial school which include the need to recognise the distinction between the *practice* of collective decision-making and the legal position of the hand.

A third point reflected uncertainty about teacher autonomy if collective decision-making was a prerequisite for creativity:

In the literature on the creative school, there is a degree of ambivalence as to the autonomy of the teacher. It is often applauded as a necessary precondition of creativity, but the autonomy of the individual teacher is, in fact, under pressure in current developments. It is obviously important that the teacher should enjoy freedom from close supervision if he is to be encouraged to be creative. On the other hand, the creativity of the school as an organisation assume a degree of collaboration that to some extent reduces the individual autonomy of the teacher. Since evidence on teacher satisfaction indicated that teachers value their autonomy very highly, there is the danger of a loss of satisfaction which needs careful consideration.

Thus the conclusions of this comparative study were similar to those provided by the national context, and support the idea that the internal arrangements in a school—the climate of relationships between teachers, and their attitudes to authority and autonomy—are more critical to the success of school-based curriculum development than, within limits, the external factors of staffing levels, administration and resource allocation.

Value assumptions of schol-based curriculum development

It is now possible to summarise the preceding argument by identifying three main features of school-based curriculum development in primary schools. First, it involves teachers in a more *collaborative role* with other teachers, working together to reconstruct, through informed discussion and critical appraisal, general curricular guidance into specific school-wide policy and practice. The process turns teachers into educationalists. Second, it involves teachers drawing upon the *specialist expertise* of curriculum postholders in order to improve existing practice and policy in a small-scale, gradualist fashion, with an openness to evaluation. Third, *internal relationships* as perceived by teachers, especially relationships resting upon authority in respect of the curriculum and classroom autonomy, are critical to the kind of developments being encouraged.

When summarised in the above way, school-based curriculum development can be seen to embody something more than advice about how change *can* occur - about mechanisms of change. It embodies a set of professional and moral values - what kinds of change *should* occur, and how they should be brought about.

This point has been explored in a particularly sharp way by Henderson and Perry, who argue that curriculum development involves what is referred to as 'organisation development'. By this they mean three things. First, the curriculum cannot be treated on its own, as a separate entity unrelated to the school as a whole, which is an integrated social system. Developing the curriculum means developing the school, especially the staff. Second, a static, mechanistic organisation is inappropriate for a changing society, which requires organisational structures and relationships that are dynamic, responsive and organic. Third, development occurs through a 'process of education and re-education', in which all those involved, not just the senior staff, are themselves continually learning.

The concept...should not imply the responsibility for initiating and organising staff development belongs *solely* to the head and senior staff, that they alone are capable of determining what is best for staff. If the head and his senior lieutenants decide upon school needs and the kind of professional development necessary to meet them, this becomes another type of 'top-downwards' model..It is not appropriate to an organic social system, where development depends upon shared responsibility for mutually agreed goals, based on sensitive understanding of the needs of the system as a whole.

Although Henderson's and Perry's discussion is mainly concerned with the appropriateness of different organisational structures for effecting change in schools, it does highlight the moral dimensions of curriculum development - the idea that some ways of introducing change are better from a moral point of view, as well as from considerations of their effectiveness for bringing about change. For school-based curriculum development in primary schools, two such value assumptions need to be articulated, even if briefly. They refer to two characteristics identified in the practice of the inquiry schools: *collaboration and subject expertise.*

One useful way into the question of value assumptions is to ask what benefits would accrue to a school in which staff collaboration and subject expertise were key characteristics in the processes by which the curriculum was developed. There might be five such benefits - three concerned with staff collaboration and two with subject expertise - which are offered here as a kind of morale criterion reference list.

Staff collaboration

(a) Curriculum policy and practice would be arrived at through collective discussion and decision-making.

(b) Initiative and responsibility for developing the curriculum would be devolved to relevant staff groups.

(c) Staff groups would be led and serviced by the postholder acting as 'educationalist'.

Subject expertise

(a) Greater continuity and consistency in the subject throughout the school would be practised.

(b) Class teachers would have enhanced respect for the postholder's expertise in his or her subject and increase their own confidence and competence in it.

When the benefits claimed for it are stated in this way, two value positions underlying school-based curriculum development can be confronted by teachers who engage in it. The first position is fairly easily expressed. It is morally desirable that a curriculum policy and the school-wide practice that flows from it—the curriculum as experienced in the classroom by children—should be based as firmly as possible in specialised expertise. Consistency in curriculum practice is only valuable in so far as it is consistently right, not wrong. Similarly, increasing teachers' confidence in a subject, and increasing their respect for a postholder's expertise, are worth while only if such confidence and respect are justified.

The second value position is that decisions developed collaboratively, and taken collectively, are arrived at by a morally better process than those arrived at by other means. The position is derived from respect to be attached to teachers as people and professionals; decisions designed to affect the personal and professional life of teachers in school should be developed only through a process in which their responsibility and commitment are recognised and explicitly acknowledged. To avoid the process, inherently difficult as it will be, would be to treat teachers with something bordering on contempt.

There is, as Hargreaves has hinted, the danger that a rhetoric of grass-roots democracy and participation might provide a distraction from the conventional exercise of undelegated authority both inside and outside the school. This is a constant danger in a profession that has been schooled to defer to authority as well as to exercise it. However, it will be lessened if the teachers involved in school-based approaches to the curriculum acknowledge and confront the values upon which it operates.

If these values are to become palphable and authentic in the life of primary schools, curriculum postholders will play a central part. It is from them that expertise will have to come: they will literally, as well as formally, have a special responsibility for their subject. they will have to be, or become, the resident 'expert', responsive to other teachers' needs. Likewise, collective decision-making needs to be efficiently led, serviced and informed by them. Thus school-based curriculum development raises fundamental questions of value for all the staff in a school -

questions of the value to be placed on specialist expertise and group decision-making in the school, and the inherent challenge that both pose to conventional claims of classroom autonomy. The implications for the 'management' of curriculum development in primary schools were discussed, but for curriculum postholders they offer an interesting, challenging and possibly daunting extension to their professional life.

6 One Approach to Primary Education: An Enabling Curriculum

For each school, each class, each child, somebody has to decide on one approach to primary education which will be, on some set of criteria, suitable. In some societies the choice is made centrally; in some, within individual schools; or in individual class; which is not the same thing. At whatever level the choice is to be made, a process of choice is necessary, and in this chapter an attempt is made to indicate how a process of choice can be applied to the three elements of development, experience and curriculum in order to derive one legitimate approach, and to indicate how others might be derived.

To do so implies an avowed choice of a set of values; or rather, it assumes that a set of values has already been chosen. No education is possible without a set of values, and any education which purports to be value-free is likely to be based on hidden values of its own. Similarly, any approach to education which claims to be entirely derived from theories of development, or experience, or of curriculum is unlikely to be adequate. For either it is based on a fallacious argument, such as that because education is related to development, therefore education ought to depend on development: or it is based on an argument derived from other and still more basic premises. The approach indicated in the present chapter is not a finely wrought, philosophically complete exposition. It rests simply on one basic assumption.

This assumption is that democratic attitudes are preferable to other attitudes. More explicitly, this means that decisions negotiated within groups are preferable to decisions imposed by superiors; that individual views should not be submerged by group views; and that no group should impose itself by any kind of force on any other group. Such a set of values is somewhat idealistic as well as being somewhat imprecise; but it does have meaning and is clearly distinguishable from authoritarian attitudes.

This basic assumption is reinforced by two others. One of these is derived from the Judaic-Christian tradition. It implies a way of valuing people which can and indeed must transcend the democratic stance, but is here regarded as fully compatible with it and adding something to it, something which at the least implies a kind of compassionate concern. The remaining assumption is simply that all unbridled ideological positions are in themselves dangerous. At the least, they imply a claim to certainty; at the most, they lead people to claim powers over others that are quite incompatible with the first two assumptions. Moreover, ideological programmes are almost always pretentious and fallacious, and when their feet of clay appear, their adherents are left adrift and bewildered.

It will, of course, be claimed that this position is itself ideological; but that is not so within the meaning given here to ideology. My position is one that is continually corrigible in its own terms, adjusting to different ideas and new emphases within the democratic framework, and finding new ways of valuing people in a compassionate way.

It may also be claimed that this position is outmoded, even disproved. In 1983 there are political currents on both Right and Left which regard this types of democratic attitude as context-bound, described, blind to stark economic, political or social realities. That is why liberal and 'social-democratic' are often use as pejoratives far beyond their standpoint as outmoded or incapable of leading to a somewhat juster social order. Rather, I think it is one the least unlikely means of attaining a somewhat juster social order. At the same time, as a Christian, I do not believe that any secular stance can in itself hold the key to social perfectibility.

With this in mind, it is possible to look again at development, experience and curriculum, to bring them together into a coherent approach to primary education.

First, the relative roles and importance of development and experience have to be judged. Development, in its three aspects can be taken as anything from a set of negative limitations, reluctantly acknowledged, to a source of guidance, uncritically accepted. From the point of view enunciated in this chapter, development has to be regarded as something positive. Individual children do each have some inbuilt programme, and each programme is different. This can be deduced from principles of heredity, but also from observation. An attempt to impose a uniform, or even a nonuniform, pattern of education that does not take serious account of developmental considerations violates any concept of democracy as it has been described here.

Experience can be taken as implying anything from the unpredictable partner of development in an interactive process to a *tabula rasa* from which heredity can be, for all practical purpose, expunged. From the point of view enunciated in this chapter, the second of the possibilities has some emotional appeal, but it is contrary to much of the evidence that arises from direct observation as well as from systematic study. The limits of experience have to be undue emphasis on its potential can easily involve brash attempts to re-mould individuals and societies, disregarding both the evidence in favour of developmental factors and the strains and misfortunes resulting for individuals when those factors are disregarded. On the other hand, over-emphasis on the inevitability of some features of development can result in a belittling of the power of experience to effect any real change, so that those who are alleged to benefit from the developmental advantages drawn from their innate endowment may continue to do so. Thus, a democratic approach requires caution in the face of either extreme view of experience.

When primary education is considered in particular, development and experience both claim consideration. Both appear with more clarity than in secondary or tertiary education, where questions of content and organization so readily tend to supervene. Young children's development is to palpable; their experience so relatively uncomplicated. What is more, the mutual dependence of development and experience is shown with particular clarity. The third element, curriculum, should thus be approached on the further assumption that *there should be a balanced interaction between development and experience*. However, that does not mean that there should be some precise Newtonian calculation of their relative importance. The balance refers not to a once-for-all weighting of their significance, but to a continuing process which gives the predominance now to the one, now to the other, in particular situations, but which is directed in the long run to the best outcome for each individual child. It also implies a re-assertion of the obvious but frequently overlooked truth that the interaction between development and experience begins before curriculum, continues alongside curriculum, and extends beyond curriculum. Moreover, curriculum, though it builds upon experience and constitutes that part of experience that falls within formal education, is still only a part of experience.

The role of curriculum considered in the rest of this book is that it is *planned intervention in the interaction between development and experience*. This is to be taken to mean that curricular experience is planned intervention between development and general experience. For the sake of simplicity, henceforth the nicety of meaning will be overlooked and 'experience' will denote 'general experience' while 'curriculum' will be used a shorthand for 'curricular experience'. In other words, the relationship spelled out will be borne in mind while a simplified terminology is used.

If the terminology is kept simple, the relationships are far from simple. For there is an ongoing interaction between the development and curriculum, and between experience and curriculum, as well as between development and experience. The difference between curriculum and the other elements is the obvious one, that development and experience are continuous, whereas curriculum is substantially confined to the place and time of formal education. This does not mean that its importance is proportionately reduced. The pressures of society throw into relief what goes on in school; curriculum as a whole, unlike development or experience as a whole, is designed to make a positive impact on children; and curriculum is fashioned in such a way as to interact positively with development and experience and to maximise their value for children.

As we have already seen, many of the most

far-seeing among those who emphasise the importance of development in education stress, as Montessori did, the necessity of curriculum as a means of optimising development. Similarly, many of the ablest and most thoughtful advocates of experience in education stress that curriculum is itself a major component of experience. As Dewey said of education: 'It is that reconstruction or reorganization of experience which adds to experience, and which increases ability to direct the course of subsequent experience'. Thus curriculum is both a part of experience and a means of extending experience.

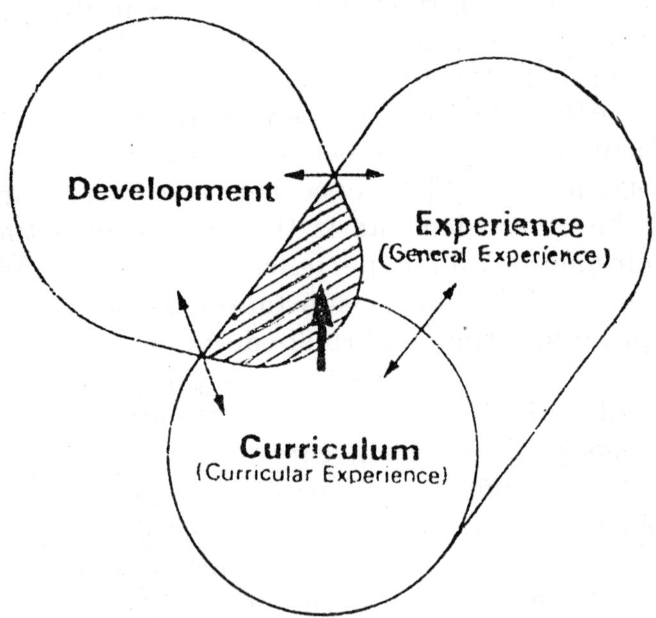

Static relationship between development, experience and curriculum

In fact, curriculum is essential to both development and experience. This is an essential part of the point of view advocated in this chapter. The relationship between the three elements can be epitomised in the model.

But of course the process is a dynamic sequence, and may perhaps be more appropriately illustrated in the form of a highly formalised flow chart. In Fig. stands for steps in development for episodes in experience; and for units of curriculum.The use of the zero subscript in the developmental and experimental series but not in the curricular series is deliberate: it emphasises that development and experience are active before curriculum begins. Similarly, if the series is continued to the end of formal education the final curriculum unit might be entitled but there would be after that continuing throughout life.

Of course, this whole diagram is immensely simplified. All sort of development and experience, and many curriculum units, are in play simultaneously. I am quite aware of this. But there are times when a concentrated notation can convey the essence of a process.

It is necessary now to turn back to the three main approaches to curriculum discussed in the previous chapter, in order to consider which of them is most promising for the purpose of planned intervention in the interaction between development and experience.

The curricular principal least appropriate for this purpose is the one derived from social imperatives. A democratic approach cannot envisage children as primarily operatives or as voters, soldiers, parishioners or even as citizens. Yet it is not as simple as this. A democratic education must at least try to ensure the conditions in which it can exist. It may permit the attachment of individuals to certain social, political or religious creeds, each of which would wish to act as the cuckoo in the democratic nest; but it cannot encourage this process or even regard it with indifference. Some positive emphasis on democratic values and their cultivation is a minimum requirement. It is a far cry from the contrived insistence on unquestioning acceptance of any one creed.

There is also another way in which the social-imperatives approach cannot be dismissed too lightly. There is a reciprocal relationship between society and formal education which goes beyond the transmission of ideas. In the accountability formulation that has become familiar in recent times, no society can live beyond its means, or will into being an educational provision or policy and administratively. The importance of economic activity can claim inclusion in a curriculum for this reason alone. On the other hand, it is unreasonable to maintain that its inclusion should take the form of prescriptive initiation into particular skills and activities without reference to the general social order within which they are to be conducted, or to some consideration of how that social order could be criticised and ameliorated.

On a smaller scale, local communities can make claims of their own. Indeed, when local communities are in a situation of particular social malaise, for example through depopulation or unemployment, a curriculum that attempts to disregard these circumstances might well be in its turn disregarded. Similarly, there may be specific claims for curricular adjustment in rural areas, or those with particular problems of bilingualism or a mix of cultures. All of these circumstances represent social imperatives of one kind or another, and all present much the same curricular dilemma. If too little notice is taken of those circumstances, the curriculum may prove irrelevant or even unworkable; if too much notice is taken of them, it may act as a means of reinforcing the separateness of the local community from the wider society and even as an obstacle in the path of those who would like to transcend its barriers and to take part in the wider society.

The social-imperatives approach does, therefore, make considerable demands upon any democratic approach to primary education. However, the positive importance of the forms and process approaches is greater.

The forms approach, in its stronger embodiment, makes claims almost irrespective of development and experience, claims derived from a totally objective view of knowledge and endeavour. But in its more flexible form it looks upon curriculum as consisting of broad areas of understanding and endeavour which have emerged within the historic process in almost all societies, certainly within those which today have established systems of formal education. This more flexible version of the forms approach does not make elaborate claims for the individual forms, nor for their precise definition, but it does assert that they are fundamentally distinct ways of understanding and endeavour, the omission of any one of which would impoverish education. This is a little less forceful than the argument based on initiation or on civic need, but it does imply that personal development and the expansion of experience require some exposure to all of them. Moreover, there is a sense in which they can claim to be themselves a part of the structure of development and experience.

However the main emphasis has to be laid on the third approach to curriculum, the process approach. This is because if the purpose is to uphold individuals and their autonomous fulfilment, then what matters is how they discover understanding and endeavour for themselves. To combine this with a flexible version of the forms is not a contradiction. The particular acts of co-operative learning and endeavour involved in the various elements in the curriculum can, and should, be based on ways of discovery that are related to development and experience. The choice of curricular areas, or indeed to the possible range of problems and activities within them, cannot be left entirely to an arbitrary process of discovery which, in practice, is often devoid of purposive sequence and structure or of the expertise needed to guide, interpret and stimulate that discovery. In other words, at the level of micro-planning of individual episodes of learning, the process approach makes strong demands: at the level of macro-planning of curriculum, it requires interaction with forms, and to some extent with social imperatives.

There is one further important consideration. In the preceding discussion there was some danger of regarding the curriculum as static, or at any rate of giving priority to the curriculum as it appears at the later primary stage. But primary education has to be considered as a whole, and begins at a chronological age when, on any showing, development and experience preclude the clear differentiation of the curriculum into forms. To begin with, it must be much more of a totality. Differentiation into separate kinds of activity is itself a part of the curriculum process at the primary stage. More than that, it is something that forms part of guided discovery. For this reason the emphasis on the process approach to curriculum at the primary stage, is further strengthened. Whatever augments might be applied in secondary or even in later primary education: the primary curriculum as a whole has to take account of what happens at the very start.

Hitherto some of the characteristics of a worthwhile primary curriculum have been indicated: its relation to development and experience, its prime but not exclusive dependence on the process model, and its modification according to age. It has already been defined as a balanced intervention in the interaction between development and experience, with the proviso that the interaction takes place between all three elements. What is needed now, before the discussion is taken further, is a more succinct term for the kind of curriculum that is to be elaborated.

If we are to speak of an enabling curriculum, them it is necessary to say what it enables, and why it enables more than would be the ease if it were not introduced.

The verdict about what this curriculum enables must depend on the approach that been advocated in this chapter. Thus, forest, it has to be a curriculum that enables development and experience to take place beneficially. It must prove additional equipment that arises through development beyond the powers of the human organism as such development that can arise only through the stimulus of a systematic process of construction of reality strengthened by awareness of widely accepted forms of understanding and endeavour. It must also provide opportunities for the expansion and reflective scrutiny of experience, within a social context that ensures that development and experience are social as well as individual.

Beyond this, it must also enable each individual to become a person with an emerging set of values and ideals. Development and experience do not necessarily imply this, so if it is a desirable goal it must fall to the enabling curriculum to promote it. Of course, the emerging set of values and ideals must itself reflect the general present purposes a democratic one, designed tc function within the various contexts that have been considered. A curriculum designed to operate within a quite different framework of values might also be termed 'enabling', but if this were to apply where only a forms approach, or a social-imperatives approach, was adopted, then its enablement would be much more limited in scope. I would be less productive, and less democratic, in its interaction with development and experience in general.

Even so, an enabling curriculum envisages two further outcomes. First, it does not simply condition development and experience, within however congenial a context. Based as it is on chosen values, it also enables choices to be made. Choices have to be made in any life situation, and choices made in the light of development and of experience are usually more widely made than those made, as it were, at random. An enabling curriculum is intended to go beyond this again.

It is intended to reveal more clearly the conditions within which choices have to be made, and the influences which bear upon the chooser. Having stripped off much of the surrounding opacity, it leaves the chooser and the choice face to face. Then, the chooser depends on the emerging set of values and ideals. For it is the ultimate strength, as well as the perversity, of personal autonomy that choices must eventually be made without dictation. In a democratic ideology, autonomy and not automation must be the intention, and the curriculum must enable but not compel. The most that enabling curriculum can do is to leave the doors and the options open: this it should do, and it is great deal to do.

Secondly, an enabling curriculum must enable *acceptance*. This may seem to contradict the enablement of choice, but in fact it places choice in perspective. It is not false humility or social quietism, but a recognition that, in our existential situation, individuals must accept limitations, not least in themselves. It sets in perspective the aim often suggested for education, that all children should be capable. For such an aim can be achieved only if it includes the power of acceptance of limitations, constrains, frustrations, disappointments, betrayals, accidents, illnesses, disasters and deaths. It may be unfashionable to emphasis this, but a curriculum that has nothing to say to these experiences, in the fact of which development usually also remains silent, is a disabling mockery. Too often, primary education has been envisaged for an unreal world created by wishful-thinking adults who prefer to sweep the unpleasant and the tragic, vicariously, under the carpet while claiming that in doing so they are 'protecting' children. A truly enabling curriculum has to enable those who meet it in the interaction between development and experience to accept reality in all its ugliness as well as all its beauty and potential.

Before the argument is taken further, it would be useful to indicate bow this enabling curriculum relates to some terms which are more familiar in discussions of the primary curriculum. One of these is *progressive*. The enabling approach has much in common with the manifestation of progressive education, whose opponents might well assume that it is little more than a variant on that theme. But the usual contention of advocates of progressive education is that it should be more self-consciously linked with children's active learning and also with a mildly socialist orientation generally. The commitment of an enabling approach to forms of understanding might also be viewed with some suspecision. Much the same might be true of the term *child-centred*. An enabling curriculum is intended to be more than child-centred. It takes account also of differences in social situation, and here again the acceptance of forms of understanding may act as a mark of distinction between an enabling and a child-centred approach. At first these distinctions may seem trivial and tedious, but they do in fact embody quite an important distinction between the typical embodiment of educational reformism and what is recommended here. For in the enabling curriculum the process approach has the principal, but not the only, place. In the remainder of this book an attempt will be made to use a consistent terminology about the enabling curriculum, even if it sometimes involves a tendency to be repetitive.

There will certainly be objections to this enabling curriculum, especially perhaps from those who are sincerely convinced of the primary of forms of understanding and endeavour as such, and of the predominant significance of subjects and disciplines. Almost as many objections could be raised by those who, from whatever point of view, accord first place to social imperatives. There will also be others, of a philosophical cast of mind, who will contend that this enabling curriculum may not in fact do the enabling that is expected of it, and that other types of curriculum might in fact be found to do the enabling at least as well, or even better. They may maintain that it represents just the kind of wishful and soft-centred extrapolation from selected research findings and from edited experience that has plagued English primary education ever since Plowden, modified only by a touch of existentialist pessimism. Still others will cavil at the mixture of forms and process that is advocated, and may wish to substitute something more sturdy and homogeneous; this position might be adopted by Blenkin and Kelly with their radical empiricist model, or by Egan with his essentially developmental approach, or by those such as Kirby who adhere more closely to the child-centred tradition. Much that is advocated in this enabling curriculum corresponds to the central tenets of one or more of these approaches, so that they are more likely to criticise it for lack of clarity and homogeneity—a curricular fudge-and-mudge, an embodiment of Richard's 'liberal pragmatism'—than to regard it as embodying that spirit of reaction. Certainly, it would gain if upheld by empirical verification, which would be a lengthy and complex business. In default of such confirmation, it is presented as a relatively appropriate way of intervening beneficially in the interaction between development and experience. What is more, it tallies with much that Richards calls for in his advocacy of a well-grounded, 'fine-grained' curriculum consistency.

7 The Teacher and the Ethos of the School

As soon as any visitor enters a school they will be aware of a feeling or atmosphere. Messages will be picked up from the state and style of the buildings, the arrangement of furnishings, the displays on the wall and labels and notices around the school. But the most significant messages will come from the behaviour of the people involved: from the welcome received from the staff, the demeanour of the children and the behaviour of staff and children towards each other. With further acquaintance, messages will be received about the quality of the teacher's attitude to parents, their expectations of children in terms of work and behaviour and numerous other aspects of school life.

Together these are many other messages will create a 'feeling' which is clearly recognized by all those involved in the school. This feeling may be described as the 'ethos' of the school, although people working in the school may characterized it in many different ways.

The term 'ethos' thus describes an aspect of school life, the reality and importance of which will be recognized by most people who have been involved in schooling. However, the 'reality' of the ethos of a school is essentially a social construction. This raises issues which will be considered in this chapter. Ethos involves a climate that permeates and affects all aspects of the school. What then are the ingredients which together create this climate? Does the answer lie in the relationships between the people who work in the school, the head, the teachers, the children, ancillary staff and visitors? What influences do the physical surroundings, the material resources available, the school's location, the Local Education Authority, have on the school? Do wider factors such as the national economic and political situation or the prevailing social and educational ideologies also have significant effects?

Why is ethos important?

Perhaps one of the most influential pieces of research into the concept of 'ethos' was undertaken by Rutter *el al*. during the 1970s. This was a longitudinal study of 5485 children in the Inner London Educational Authority (ILEA) who were followed from their primary schools through five years of secondary schooling. They found that the differences in the schools' intakes could not explain the differences between outcomes when the children were fourteen. Schools with similar intakes seemed to produce very different results. The Rutter team put these differences in outcome down to differences in 'ethos' among the schools.

More effective schools appear to be those

which function as a coherent whole, with staff at all levels supporting each other and working towards shared academic and social goals. In such schools, senior staff give a clear lead and at the same time teachers feel views are represented.

Thus, Rutter's work indicates that the ethos of a school is important because it is positively related to educational outcomes.

Unfortunately Rutter's 'outcomes' do not necessarily define the purposes of schooling and some outcomes such an examination performance and rates of delinquency may have little relevance to the primary schools. Others may not be among the priorities even of secondary schools. The Rutter research did not explore process such as curriculum development or the willingness of the staff and head to innovate. In the more child-centred primary sector these may be more important aspects. In addition, in a primary school the children themselves may have a greater effect on the 'ethos' of the school than Rutter suggests. However, despite these and other criticisms, Rutter found much evidence that some schools seem to have consistently better outcomes than others and this is largely a result of shared rules, standards and values of those within the school.

The findings of Reynolds support the view that a positive climate is an important factor in school effectiveness. He found that the school's policy towards children is of central importance. A climate where children feel they are part of decision making, the school social structure, rather than being coerced, produces higher educational achievement. In such schools, teachers value and reward academic achievement and 'humanistic' activity.

Brookover *et al.* also found that attitudes to children are influential on academic achievement. In effective schools there is an assumption that the children are willing and able to learn and very few are 'written off'. In an ineffective school the same children would be classified as slow and unable to learn:

> We therefore conclude that a school's social climate and the instructional behaviours associated with it are more direct causal links in the production of achievement behaviour in reading and mathematics than socio-economic and racial variables.

A criticism of these studies when applying their findings in the primary school context is that much of the work was undertaken in secondary schools. Outcomes that were measured in some cases seem 'mechanistic' and outside of the more 'romantic' primary tradition and concerns. However, there has been a more recent project looking at the effectiveness of 50 ILEA primary schools which discovered that some schools were more effective than others in promoting pupils' learning and development, and also in catering for particular groups of children such as boys or girls, and children from different social classes and ethnic groups. In the study, account was taken of variations in the pupils' background. Twelve factors were found to influence the effectiveness of the school. The schools which produced a positive ethos had the following characteristics:

1. Purposeful leadership by the headteacher. Headteachers were actively involved in the school's work, without exciting *total* control.
2. Involvement of the deputy head. Headteachers shared and delegated some of their responsibilities. Frequent absence of the deputy was detrimental to pupil progress.
3. Involvement of teachers. Teachers were involved in curriculum planning, guidelines development and decision making.
4. Consistency among teachers. Teachers were consistent in the use of guidelines.
5. Structured sessions. Teachers organized pupils' work programmes and gave them plenty to do. Once work had been allocated, pupils were encouraged to work independently.
6. Intellectually challenging teaching. Teachers used higher-order questions and statements, encouraging pupils to solve problems and use creative imagination.
7. Work-centred environment. Classrooms were busy and purposeful with teachers spending time discussing the content of work rather than routine issues. Pupils appeared to enjoy their work and were keen to start new work. Classrooms were reasonably quiet and without excessive movement.

8. Limited focus within sessions. Teachers concentrated on one or two curriculum areas in any session. All pupils were not, however, doing the same work and teachers geared the work to pupils' needs.

9. Maximum communication between pupils and teachers. This was achieved by the teacher talking more often to the whole class or groups rather than to individuals. This enabled 'higher order' communication to occur more often.

10. Record keeping. Teachers kept good records of planning and assessment of pupils' personal, social and development work.

11. Parental involvement. Schools and an informal open-door policy with parents helping in the classroom and on visits and régular meetings organized to discuss pupils' progress. Parents were involved in pupils' educational development. The mere fact of having a formal parent-teacher association was not sufficient to promote a positive ethos.

12. Positive climate. The emphasis within the schools was on praise and encouragement rather than criticism and punishment. There was firm but fair classroom management with teachers having a positive attitude to their classes and taking an interest in all aspects of the children.

They organized trips and lunchtime and after-school clubs. The teachers had good working conditions and timetabled non-teaching periods.

The researchers point out that these factors cannot constitute a complete 'recipe' for promoting pupil learning but may provide a framework within which school effectiveness and its relationship to ethos may be considered.

It is interesting to note that many of the factors identified in the ILEA study are similar to those found by earlier studies to contribute to the ethos of a school. This is important because effectiveness may require a different definition at primary level and the definitions may change alongside altering perceptions of the role of the primary school. At this level it may be necessary as Golby says, to ask new questions such as whether the school's purposes are in line with those of parents, pupils and society. It is not possible to assume that the conventional school curriculum is consistent with those purposes. Gray points out other questions that are relevant in the primary school context. For instance, measures of effectiveness can only be used with confidence if schools are stable from year to year and they enable educational practitioners to identify more effective schools. We need tc know whether the effects of 'ethos' are greater or less at primary level. It is important to know how the 'ethos' of a school becomes established and whether, as Frances believes, process interacts with outcomes to produce a spiral effect, rather than a directly causal effect on outcomes,

What does seem apparent from the research referred to above and from work by others such as McDill, Webber, Madden and Brookover and

Lezotte, is that there are combinations of factors, which may be termed 'ethos', that have profound effects on pupil performance.

In teasing out the factors that affect the ethos of schools it is apparent that management has a great influence. Central to this is the relationship that exists between the headteacher and staff. Indeed the DES Report of 1977 states that the headteacher is the most important factor in the climate of a school.

How does management contribute to ethos?

Research indicates that effective headteachers are sympathetic, empathetic and accessible. Nias found that such headteachers set clear aims for the school that are subject to negotiation within limits. The capacity to create cohesion and to support and encourage individuals is essential. This is likely to be enhanced by the head's own high standard of personal commitment and professional competence.

Simon identifies two leadership styles which may be adopted by headteachers. The first involves the use of influence. such headteachers seek to understand problems thoroughly in order to arrive at the right line of action. This involves an appeal to expertise and obtaining the consent of staff to proposed developments. The second involves the use of control, the exercise of authority to obtain the acquiescence of staff through a mixture of threat and persuasion. Management that relies on control may divide staff and invite confrontation or passive resistance. Bolam and Pratt point out that controllers may adopt strategies that involve the use of incentives as well as sanctions. If compliance is forced it may result in low staff morale and lack of effort. Such a headteacher is likely to lose the confidence of staff. Ballinger found that at the extreme such headteachers may use autocratic strategies of lying, rigging agendas or altering information in order to deny or exclude opposing ideas.

Blake and Mouton found that school management s may be more or less focused on social satisfaction or task achievement. School managements which focus on neither may be described as impoverished. Those that focus on social satisfaction to the exclusion of task achievement may be described as 'Country Clubs', pleasant places to work achievement do so at the expense of the social and emotional development of teachers and children. The ideal, of course, is to focus on both aspects. Most schools focus more on one aspect or the other at different times.

Mile's model of 'organizational health' sought to identify dimensions of effective management. He grouped ten dimensions of organizational health under three main headings. Two of these, task-centred and maintenance needs, are closely related to those identified by Blake and Mouton but he adds a third, growth and changefulness. Miles's dimensions are as follows:

Task-centred

(a) *Goal focus*: goals should be clear, accepted, realistic and achievable.

(b) *Optimal power equalization*: teachers motivated by feelings of involvement and competence.

(c) *Communication adequacy*: vertical and horizontal lines of communication should be open, easy and distortion free.

Maintenance needs

(a) *Cohesiveness*: clear sense of identity which is attractive to teachers.

(b) *Morale*: well-being, laughter, lack of stress.

(c) *Resource utilization*: resources should be co-ordinated so that teachers are working hard, in jobs they suit but are not stressed.

Growth and changefulness

(a) *Innovativeness*: growth and development, increase in range of school's and teacher's activities.

(b) *Autonomy*: staff respond to, but not be dictated to, by pressures from outside.

(c) *Problem-solving adequacy*: problems identified, solved and evaluated with minimum stress.

(d) *Adaption*: strength and stability in order to allow for faster change.

It is often assumed that a headteacher likely to foster organizational health might be described as democratic. However, Crick believes that democracy does not provide a good model for effective management. Its meaning is too uncertain. It may mean majority rule, or the will of the staff, or 'one-person-one vote' or the pursuit of equality. It is not a suitable model for school management, where all decisions cannot be taken by the whole staff. In a democracy, general interests may be taken into account but minority interests may be ignored. To manage well, headteachers may have to go against popular opinion and desirable goals may be mutually exclusive. Crick saw a political style of leadership as more appropriate, in which teachers' and children's interests are represented and communication is open but were the headteacher may take a wider view.

Hoyle described the micropolitics of school management in which groups within the staff may co-operate to achieve a common goal. Such groupings may be *ad hoc* or formal and may be committed to preserving the *status quo*. Such groupings may lead to the 'dark underworld' of illegitimate micropolitics which include power broking and closed political processes. Marsh and Olsen describe how decisions may be made before consultation and negotiation and history 'rewritten' to make the process appear more rational.

Handy describes how groups, whether legitimate or illegitimate, provide a psychological home for individuals by providing institutional and individual functions. Individual functions include the satisfaction of social needs, such as self-esteem, support and sharing. Institutional functions include management needs such as problem-solving, information collection and processing co-ordination, commitment, negotiation and enquiry. Beneficial functioning of groups occurs where relations between individuals at all levels are good. Ideas are better evaluated and involvement is increased. This can lead to a positive cycle being established where greater productivity leads to more satisfaction, which in turn leads to still greater productivity.

In this process Richardson emphasized the importance of open and honest communication. This is only possible if the headteacher communicates trust in the teachers' abilities to educate children. When this trust is built up teachers can risk exposing problems and revealing weaknesses and so develop their skills. A warm and accepting atmosphere is necessary before staff can examine what is good and bad in their school. The fostering of delusions, or suffocation of conflicting ideas beneath a veneer of politeness, will tend to mask problems. This can produce the problem of the preservation of hormony becoming an end in itself, resulting in a resistance to any change in the *status quo*. Beeby pointed out the importance of an honest questioning and examination of behaviour and values that had to be taken for granted. Planning in education is not purely objective but involves value systems and attitudes which need to be discussed. Having been implemented, change should be subject to criticism and feedback. This is only possible where teachers feel their interests are taken into account and there is communication between all levels of staff. An autocratic headteacher will invite confrontation or passive resistance. Such a head will be denied feedback from the teachers in the school and the opportunity to improve planning in the light of experience. The teachers are unlikely to experience support from the headteacher or the satisfaction of a task well done with the consequence of low morale. The headteacher's role within an effective school is thus very demanding and diffuse, in order to produce a climate where problems may be solved in cooperation. The headtechers mush initiate change and motivate staff by example and consideration.

What factors inhibit the development of a positive ethos?

I have discussed research findings which identify positive and negative factors within schools which affect the development of ethos. However, I would argue that in today's economic and political climate there are many pressures outside schools' control which may inhibit the development of positive ethos.

Education takes place in a politicized context, with all the implications that has for accountability. In the context of the 1988 Education Reform Act Schools can no longer ignore the community in which they work. Parents will be closely involved in the management of schools and decisions over opting out. In addition schools will operate in a 'market place' where they must attract 'customers' and satisfy those they have already attracted. This is, however, not just a new phenomenon. Government reports from Plowden through to recent reports such as

Warnock have emphasized the need for parental involvement in primary schools. This has led to a much greater openness but also to the development of tensions. The school has to become more explicit about its aims, and these may be challenged by parents who do not feel them to be in tune with their needs and purposes. Problems may become more acute with the publication of schools' assessment results. At the same time as schools are responding to parents' interests and needs, they are under pressure from government and local authority expectations. Those of central government have become very detailed and explicit and may conflict in some respect with its previous policies and philosophy of the Local Education Authority. the resolution of these tensions can lead to real progress, but in order for this to happen the pacing and timing of change needs careful consideration. Unfortunately this does not always appear to be the case Even before the Education Act headteachers and teachers felt pressured by the sheer number of new initiatives that they were invited, or pressed to participate in. These arrived from a variety of sources, each convinced that their concerns should receive priority. the HMI document on the curriculum from 5 to 16 years states.

Schools will necessarily have to take account of the policy decisions of LEAs and central government and of the expectations of parents, employers and the community at large... schools also have to respond to social changes, to the impact of technology and to changing patterns of employment ... schools have to take account of the varying concerns of all those who 'use' the system, in ways which outline the extringencies of the moment.

This thinking has been implemented by the Act. Such consideration and accountability is a tall order, especially as many of the interest groups will have conflicting concerns and requirements. At a time of low morale and declining resources the sheer weight of these demands can have profoundly inhibiting effects on the climate of schools and consequently for school effectiveness. the government in its document. *Better Schools* states:

The Government's view, following HMI reports, is that a significant number of teachers are performing below the standard required to achieve the planned objectives of schools.

Such statements, even though true in specific instances, may have a harmful effect on teacher morale, especially given the large number of aspects that schools are expected to take action on, some required by law and others a priority by influential pressure groups. The problem which confronts schools and teachers is not in the first instance the truth or otherwise of the various criticisms, or the value or otherwise of the various initiatives but rather how to handle the volume of criticism and initiatives without damaging the morale of teachers which underpins the successful ethos of schools.

There are, unfortunately, no simple solutions

to these problems. Part of the answer may, however, lie in the work that teachers do together in defining a framework for the consideration of problems and issues.

What factors inhibit the development of a positive ethos?

The ethos of a school is in large part determined by the values of those working within it. it therefore becomes necessary for teachers to discuss and analyse those values before priorities for action can properly be defined. It is important to define values within a school, because ethos is the expression of these values.

There are questions which are fundamental to any such consideration. The first is the definition of the nature of teaching. It may not be assumed that all staff share the same view of what constitutes teaching. Fox discovered that teachers defined their purposes in teaching very differently. He grouped these definitions into four main categories:

1. *Transfer:* In this model teaching is seen as the; process of transferring knowledge from one person to another. The child is seen as an empty vessel and if knowledge fails to be transferred the problem tends to be seen as residing in the child.

2. *Shaping:* Teaching is the process of moulding children to a predetermined pattern. Children are taught skills and ways of behaving which are viewed as useful in themselves. The child's interests and motives are only important in so

far as they interfere with the moulding process.

3. *Travelling:* In this model teaching is seen as a matter of guiding children through subject matter. The subject is viewed as an exciting and sometimes difficult terrain to be explored.

4. *Growing:* The focus of teaching is on the child's intellectual physical and emotional development. The teacher's job is to provide the situation and experience to assist the child in this development. This is a child-centred model, in which the subject matter is important, not as an end in itself, but only in as much as it meets the child's needs and is in the child's interest.

Each of these models has important implications for teacher action and concern and hence for the ethos of the school. Many primary school staffs would, I suspect, define their purposes in terms of 'growing'. In this case there are important factors that arise and need to be discussed in order to develop a philosophy and action that will promote a positive ethos. A staff which has defined its values and developed a philosophy of teaching will need to consider the practical implications. Below I have outlined five aspects which may be considered.

Evaluation and record keeping: If each child's interests and needs are to be met these must be accurately determined, monitored and recorded. Reliance solely on the teacher's intuition and perception is likely to produce an inaccurate picture, and a more homogeneous one than exists in reality. Teachers will therefore need to share their knowledge of individual children and together devise methods of collecting data on individual children, for instance through observation schedules, checklists, analysing children's work, individual questioning and group discussion. Records of children's development, needs and interests will have to be constantly updated. In this the TGAT report may have provided a useful way forward—but not if teachers 'teach to the tests' in order to protect themselves from criticism and fail to use the results for diagnostic purposes to improve children's learning experiences and develop their teaching.

Teaching and learning methods: In order to meet the range of individual children's needs for intellectual, physical and emotional development teachers may have to extend their range of teaching and learning methods. Many teachers rely on a relatively limited reportoire of teaching methods which are unlikely to suit the stage of development and learning style of each individual in their class, or even the different needs of any particular child meeting different subject matter or in various situations. there will therefore be a need for teachers to share expertise.

Planning: If the child rather than the subject matter is to be the focus of teaching, the planning of the curriculum purely in terms of subject matter will no longer be adequate. HMI suggest that the curriculum should also be analysed in terms of skills, attitudes, concepts and knowledge.

There is concern that the emerging reports of the national curriculum subject working parties pay insufficient attention to attitudes. The national curriculum may help to ensure continuity and coherence within the subjects but teaching may become fragmented and opportunities to reinforce learning across its curriculum may be ignored. In addition, the needs of children who do not acquire skills, concepts and knowledge in a linear way will need to be met. Teachers will need support from each other to analyse what they are doing in order to maximize the benefits of the national curriculum and minimize its defects. Curriculum planning and analysis in these terms will be new to many teachers and is likely to be difficult. Again teachers are more likely to produce flexible and effective plans which will meet the needs of all the individual children if they support and advise each other in this endeavour.

Organization: In order to meet the needs of individual children within the school, it is necessary that the staff group examines the way people, space and time are organized, including looking at them form the child's point of view. In many schools routines have been built up that may interfere with the child's needs and interests. Space may need to be reorganizsed to allow a wider variety of children's activity to co-exist. Time should also be considered, both in terms of the 'class' day and the individual child's day. For instance it is not uncommon for infant schools to 'work' in the morning and 'choose' in the afternoon on the grounds that children are a fresher in the morning. Assumptions such as this need questioning. What 'hidden' messages are being conveyed about the relative importance of different types of activity? Are the children"s needs for changes in the pace of activity within sessions being met? When teachers examine the use of time as experienced by individual children they are often surprised. A child with learning difficulties may be in a class where a wide variety of activities take place, but day after day he works so painfully slowly that he never moves on from his written work. How are this child's needs for social learning, creative expression and successfully meeting a challenge to be satisfied?

Relationship: A definition of teaching which is concerned with children's intellectual, physical and emotional development, implies a consideration of the whole child. children cannot be viewed as *tabulae rasae* when they come to school. This has implications for relationships with the community which the child comes from and especially with parents. A comparison of roles of the teacher and the parent will soon reveal much overlap. The parent and teacher will have much that is useful to offer each other. School staffs who adopt this model will have to analyse carefully their policy towards parents to discover if it is an open as possible and genuinely equal and two-way. Other schools are coming to realize the importance of partnerships and parents after the Education Reform Act more painfully. There are, however, more important reasons for the involvement of parents than the Act. Without a developing relationship with parents, teachers will be less able to understand children's cultural background and treat them with the respect they merit. Through this understanding teachers can avoid simplistic labels and stereotypes, value minority customs and focus upon what cultures have in common rather than on differences and problems. The school's policy towards children will also need to be examined to ensure that all children's needs for social satisfaction and task achievement are met and special skills or talents nurtured. The actions of teachers will need to be analysed and questioned - for instance it may be necessary to examine the experience of education offered to girls and boys respectively or children from different cultural backgrounds. In order to cater for children's emotional needs the question of motivation will need to be addressed. for instances the use of positive reinforcement may been to be monitored. Unfortunately, many primary teachers use criticism more often than praise. It may be necessary to instigate a policy of finding something of value to prise for each child every day. Methods of control by criticism may be replaced by finding the child who is working well and praising him. Work by Blanchard and Johnson points to be effectiveness of a policy of systematically 'catching children being good', which creates a more positive ethos. the type of relationships which underpin a 'growing' model of teaching can be very problematic to teachers. There is an implication of more equality between teacher, parent and child. The classroom is no longer the teacher's territory and she may have to accept parents' freer access to the room or to the child's work. In this process the support of other teachers is likely to be very necessary.

The model presented here emphasizes words such as 'share', 'support', 'collaboration' and 'relationship'. this reflects the view that the development of ethos cannot be a 'top down' activity decided by a government or the headteacher and implemented by the staff, but rather requires continual discussion and honest examination by everyone working in the school.

8 Children's Perceptions of Teachers

Children develop a clear idea of the contrast between primary schools ad secondary schools by the time they are preparing to transfer from one to the other. The picture in their mind is a universal shorthand which they all share and which reflects the way in which the two sorts of schools are contrasted, not only in how they manage the curriculum and organize the school, but in the role of teachers. Primary school children share the view that secondary schools are more important, as well as bigger and more demanding :

Girl: I think the comprehensive is the most important. Because that's where you get your 'O' levels .... it's going to be a log bigger, and the teachers are a lot stricter.

Boy: The secondary school's more important than the primary because you've got more things to learn ... There will be more classes ... bigger children ... bigger buildings.

In some ways the contrasts between primary schools and secondary schools are obvious. In primary schools children stay in one classroom, supervised by one teacher for the majority of the time. In secondary schools children go from class to class, to be taught by a variety of specialists. One result of this essential difference is that children associate primary schools with peacefulness rather than bustle, with calm rather than bullying and with close personal relationships rather than with impersonal rules.

Such a clear view of the distinct and seemingly obvious role of the primary school implies an equally marked view of primary school teachers. By contrast with the secondary school specialist, they are assumed to know everything and to be helpful in everything. But there does not seem to be the same respect attached to such helpfulness as there is to the teacher who is only seen occasionally and who is associated with one specialist subject. The view of the secondary school teacher, by children anticipating the experience, is of someone who does not pay them close attention.

Boy: I don't think I'll do that at secondary school because she might be busy and say she can't help you.

Girl: I don't think you'll have time to talk to the comprehensive teacher, because you'll be doing work and more work.

These teachers are seen to be 'strict' as well as distant, demanding more work as well as giving fewer explanations.

These anticipations heighten children's perceptions of the primary school teacher. They share a view which seems consistent despite different teaching styles. Underlying the teacher's various roles, children feel that the primary teacher is there to help, and support, and is willing to listen and explain. When children develop their sense of what makes a good teacher they often imply that the primary teachers stand, at best, for firmness of manner, ability to explain and friendliness. But as we will see, children do not necessarily *respect* those very qualities that they like. It's as if the very idea of the secondary school as a more fearful place, with bigger children, and bigger gangs, with more organized bullying, and with teachers so intent on their subject that they are indifferent to what takes place in the corridor, proved that it was more significant.

The very security that a primary school affords appears as being rather cosy to the children in their last year, as well as those in their first year at secondary school. The primary school is seen as altogether less demanding.

Girl: It teaches you the basic things before you go on to the more complicated things ... just the basic work.

Boy: It sets you up for the secondary school ... you're going to have to know about everything and there's a lot more subjects.

The primary school teacher, however, possesses particular opportunities because of the relationships which can be made. Many children respond to the idea of having the teacher as a friend.

Girl: I think I would like to have one special teacher I could be friends with.

However, children also accept that the relationship with the teacher has a professional basis. What they hope for from their classteacher is a sense of personal interest and encouragement. when children criticize the ethos of the primary school classroom, then or subsequently they single out how much depends on whether they get on with just one teacher, and how difficult it can be if they do not. In secondary school they do not feel they have to get on closely with *any* teacher. But the rewards of a good relationship with a primary school teacher are clear.

Boy: If I am worried about work I just go to the teacher and she helps me. If you get it wrong she shows you how to do it ... and then she makes jokes and tells us how to do it.

Girl: I normally go up and we talk about it and she shows me how to do it. she talks to the class as well. If so many people ask about one question she tells us all in a group. She says stop what you're doing and brings us up to the blackboard.

Children are also sensitive about whether they are liked or not; they want the teacher to 'look at you nicely' and to 'like everyone in the class'. With one or two exceptions they feel confident in their teacher because they feel understood and because they will not be rejected if they want help:

Boy: I like to have one special class teacher because she's the one main one because she knows me better.

The teacher in the classroom creates a special relationship with both the class as a whole and with individual children. Within their classroom children feel a certain sense of security.

Boy : I like to work in my own room as everybody is around you and you can hear people walking about and children talking and everything ... I won't like moving from classroom to classroom.

Girl: It's good being in the same classroom all day because you know where you are going and you get to know you classroom so you feel comfortable there.

But whilst the classroom itself seems secure, it is placed in the context of the school as a whole, and this conveys a far more authoritarian image. The teacher within the classroom might strike up a special relationship with the children, but remains the teacher, who represents a particular status and clearly defined organization. For children, school represents a series of rules, a code of discipline and a hierachical authority. Part of the security they feel derives from this sense of an imposed order. None of the children questions the need for rules. Indeed, they are adamant that on practical grounds rules are not only necessary, but become more necessary as they grow older. Without rules, children imply, there would be chaos:

Girl: If we didn't have rules we could come to school any time we wanted. If we didn't have rules you'd get up to all sorts of mischief.

Boy: If you didn't have rules in the school, everybody'll just be running riot ... they may have some kids who turn out to be really naughty, so you'll need more rules.

Children accept the authority of teachers because they see them as part of the edifice of the school, as a place where there needs to be strict control, and clear organization. Teachers need to accept this fact about their position,. even if they find it puzzling that children feel so strongly about it. They do know that they can only develop close and friendly relationships within the context of such authority. Children do not like teachers to break down the barriers of their professional status too far. Indeed, children sense the distinction between their own private lives and the kind of working relationships they develop with teachers:

Girl: I would not tell my teacher because she is not part of my home ... I don't feel I could go to any teacher if it was my own problem.

Children accept adult authority as more important than the authority of their peers, but they also accept the authority of their peers over that of adults who do not seem to them to justify, or carry out, the responsibility of authority. Teachers are therefore seen in a somewhat ambiguous light. At one level they are appreciated for their willingness to be friendly, to convey a sense of humour, and to take seriously the individual learning difficulties of children in their classroom. But this is within the context of their status, and their role within the authority of the school.

Children's perceptions of what teachers should be like derive from a set of clearly formed normative values. They are based on expectations as much as experience and are shared consistently amongst them. Children feel that teachers should be authoritarian, that they should make decisions and that they should impose order and structure. These are, of course, not the only values that children perceive in teachers, and the ways in which teachers convey such characteristics varies greatly. Nevertheless primary school teachers are seen as authoritative even if at a less exalted level that their secondary colleagues. Children respect the distance that they keep. They like to see consistency in teachers' behaviour, and this in itself implies a certain distance from children's individual needs. They do not like temporary teachers, partly because they do not know which rules have been negotiated and established. And children feel that they can get the better of teachers who become genuinely upset.

One of the essential tasks of primary teachers, which they carry out with great sophistication, is the response to *all* the children in the classroom. An experienced teacher knows instinctively whom to cajole, whom to ignore and whom to discipline when there is a sign of disorder in the classroom. But it seems that the teachers who are most closely aware of the needs of all the groups within the classroom are also those who have less highly defined authority in the children's eyes. The most authoritarian created rules and expectations into which some children could not easily fit, even if they wanted to. For children appear not only to see the teacher's role as ambiguous, as a tension between the need for control and the need for responsiveness, but to develop such a tension in their personal attitudes to teachers strongly as ordinary people, outside their role. This is one reason why secondary school teachers have higher status in their eyes. It is as if the more that primary school teachers were appreciated for their openness and concern, the less closely they filled the prevailing sense of status. Mitman, for example, found that teachers who showed concern for the slower, less gifted children were both flexible and more accurate in their assessment of children's individual abilities and needs. But these same teachers were also rated by the children as significantly lower in the quality of their teaching. It is as if quality of understanding and the ability to deliver information were not only separate, but somehow incompatible in children's eyes.

Children's views of the authority of the teacher include the acceptance that part of their role is the suppression of disorder. They are seen not only to represent authority but to impose it. Children need 'people to supervise them' and the people who do that, of course, are teachers; 'teachers are always there to tell you off and that'. The problem with children's notions that they do not have any natural tendency to behave well is that they force teachers into a role which seems alien to the children's interests. Children assume that strict discipline is necessary but they also complain that there is not enough real knowledge of children and their work displayed by teachers. Whilst the children think that their *own* individual development is most important, the teachers rate staff co-operation as the highest priority. Children do not see much of the staff as a collective group, although they are assumed to be a coherent body, all fulfilling the same role. Instead, children are aware both of their own classteacher and the distinctions between one teacher and another.

Boy: I don't like telling Mr.J. when I'm crying ... I had Miss.H. ... she was ever so kind ... Mrs W. was horrible ... she used to take it out on us.

Children's view of individual teachers are not normally so subjective. They are capable of giving a clear analysis of the teaching style, and more particularly, the teacher's attitude towards discipline. Teachers do not need reminding how acutely children observe them, and how children absorb clues from all the nuances of behaviour and language. The very way in which children are spoken to reveals what the teacher is feeling and demanding, and children find it necessary to anticipate and guess what is being expected.

Girl: If you're naughty she speaks deeply and when she looks happy she likes you. She always looks happy at me.

Boy: After a while you know what the teacher's like, and you can go up and ask them and you'll know they'll help you.

Girl: I'm quite happy here because Mrs P. likes me and she likes giving me responsibility. Thats how I know she likes me and she doesn't shout at me a lot when I've done something wrong.

The better the children are at guessing what the teacher demands, the easier they find it to accommodate to the tasks that are set them. This naturally means that some children are more adept at manipulating the circumstances to their own advantage than others. Part of the daily excitement of relationships between groups and the teacher in the primary classroom is the testing of the barrier, to see how far children can go in terms of independence or avoiding work, without causing the teachers to react. Pollard calls such children 'jokers': those who do not fit safely in the category of the obviously 'good' nor into the group which is definitely unco-operative.

The children who are best able to take advantage of the teacher are the 'brighter' ones, who both make use of the resulting freedom and make the teacher feel rewarded because they guess what is wanted. Some pupils, therefore, have more power than others over the teacher. Such power does not derive from increased demand, for in the teacher's busy day, there is a sense of relief when children are not insisting on too much help or too much work. If children were constantly demanding more, teachers could not always cope. It is as if the circumstances of the classroom made it incumbent on all the children *not* to force the pace too much, to allow for a steady work load than in the end suits both the children and the teacher.

'Brighter' children show their ability to manipulate, to guess what is wanted, and to please the teacher, even if they are not, or perhaps because they are not, working too hard. Many of these are girls. Boys and girls are aware of the distinction between teachers' attitudes toward them in the primary school, even if it is more apparent later. Just as children assume that they are all naughty and need some form of discipline, so they notice that boys are more frequently told off, and that they *need* to be. Boys tend to initiate more interactions with teachers than do girls, and this means that girls receive, in return, less response from the teachers. But then boys also receive many more negative commands and reactions that have nothing to do with work than do girls. Boys accept this as a consequence of their different behaviour patterns.

Boy: Mrs Y... likes the girls. The girls don't get started fighting and swearing. Some of the boys get your nerves on edge and you get really mad and you start saying things to them or sticking your pencil into them. Miss normally lets the girls do things like give out the books or give out the papers ... she looks angry at me. Sometimes I'm in trouble. Some of the boys just make me get

> really angry and when I try to go up and tell Miss she won't even listen or the other boys try and stop me.

Whilst children are aware of the developing difference between the sexes it is not something that figures in their attitudes towards teachers as much as in secondary school. Nor do children indicate that it matters to them whether the teacher is a man or a woman. The characteristics of the good teacher are not dependent on gender. When one boy remarks that he likes a 'man and a lady teacher but I prefer a man' it is a reflection of his attitude towards his home life: 'My Mum nags all the time ... Ladies nag at home but at school'.

The transmission of values, whether from the home, peer groups or school, is a complex matter. Teachers themselves use the way in which children see them, and their own roles, in a variety of ways. Whilst the ambiguity between their authority and their desire to help is at the heart of the way children respond to them, teachers find a variety of means to cajole children into working. they obviously succeed by taking on the attitudes and the policies of the school, standing for collective standards. But they can also withdraw from the institutional bias into a sense their own individual expertise, or their own stated expectations. They also recognize the ambiguity of their own role, just as the children experience it, as both part of a collective or group, and as an autonomous being. But, however hard teachers try to explore different kinds of relationships, and however hard they strive to create in children a sense of their own autonomy, they are faced with children's perceptions of them as people who control events. Children therefore see praise for their work as recognition that it is 'correct' and that they have discovered the way to please the teacher. They also see criticism as referring to carelessness or lack of effort, as if the work set them were tasks designed for practice rather than for originality.

However hard teachers try, children will tend to interpret their 'open' questions which demand a variety of original responses as 'closed', assuming there is just one possible answer and that any other one is wrong. Children seem to think they are learning a fixed body of knowledge. They see the teacher as the authority who knows what this is. It is not surprising that children transfer their awareness of what teachers actually intend in matters or organization and control, to the parallel circumstances of knowledge,. Teachers use language in a distinctive way in the classroom, for instance with flippant remarks and insults, which are neither meant nor recognized as such and yet would be unusual if employed elsewhere. It is as if a different code were being used, like direct questions which demand nothing but 'closed' implicit responses. 'Could you open the door?' demands an active response, not a thoughtful consideration. 'Do you know the answer?' means 'Tell me'.

Teachers' questions are perceived as purveying control and as far as the delivery of the curriculum is concerned, are assumed to be full of instructions. It is as if children assumed that the traffic of work were all one way; with them fulfilling whatever task the teacher wants, and asking the teacher only for help in carrying out that task. This is why it has been found that the teachers who actually ask most questions are least likely to receive questions back from the children. Furthermore a battery of questions, far from stimulating children into spontaneous comments or any other contributions, can actually inhibit them from work. And yet questions have an important role to play, despite the suspicions of children. For children also learn information best when they are asked about it, not just because questions are a form of testing but because children, through the teachers questions, see the information as falling into a structure that the teacher is conveying in a subtle manner. Questions are therefore not only seen as a means of conveying information but are used as a means of organizing information.

There is one way in which children feel that teachers can help; one gift that is especially appreciated. This ability goes beyond being friendly. It is the willingness and capacity to *explain*.

Girl: I like more explaining. More simple. I get stuck and muddled. Then I try to work it out and if I can't go to Mrs G—then she help me.

Most children assume that at secondary school it will be up to them to 'work' it out, but that in primary school explanations are clearly presented:

Girl: Here they explain. They explain before they've given it to you; if you don't understand you get easier work to do.

This might be interpreted as a pupil's version of 'matching' but in fact children rate the desire to know and understand what they are doing so highly that it affects whatever work they are doing. They enjoy being challenged. They are willing to try new things but want to be able to get help, preferably from the teacher, although they also get help from their friends.

Boy: We talk about the subject we are doing. If I'm stuck I put my hand up and she comes to my desk and shows me how to do it.

The willingness to be responsive to their individual needs seems to children to mark out the particular virtues of the primary school teacher. But the teacher is not only a responsive agent, waiting for clients behind the desk. She is someone seen as active in promoting clarity, and is often juxtaposed against the image of the purely distant teacher concerned that children 'get on with it' themselves by picking up information from books.

Boy: I prefer doing it with all the class than just set from a book. The teacher does it on the board and writes things and everybody gets a chance to answer them. So its not like a book when you're the only one who can try to answer them. Everybody can do it and try and I like that better.

The primary class is, after all, a collective enterprise, where children also help each other. they know that as a central organizer the teacher makes sure they all join in:

Girl: Instead of standing round the desk all the time and wasting time he reads out the answers. For marking. He gives us nice worksheets instead of using books all the time. He makes them up himself and that makes them better to do. He kind of puts them in his own words. It's easier as well.

Implicit in any analysis of work is the idea of the 'answer'; the correct response. This is true however the class is organized. The teacher needs to explain because the goal is to attain the right answer, or the right skill.

Girl: When we are finding it difficult she talks a lot to the whole class. She doesn't always talk to one person, just when they go up. If about eight people keep doing it wrong she talks to the whole classroom.

The teacher is seen to balance the needs of the individual with that of the whole class.

Boy : Well, she teachers the whole group and then she tells you on your own. she does work on the board ... if you don't understand it you can go to the teacher and talk about it. If you're just lazy she'll tell you off.

Children assume that the teacher's questions are directed towards helping them know the information, and organize the information. the kind of teacher talk that children appreciate is not the general introduction, that seems to hem to keep them awaiting before they get on with the work, but the kind which is directed towards helping them understand *how* to do the set task. The teacher is there to help them learn the *process* of work, and not just the information. Children are interested in learning the *skills* of work, and lay stress on the pleasure of being able to do the work, whilst understanding what they are doing.

Boy: Learning your tables isn't fun but doing things is.

Girl: If you still don't understand you can go up to her ... like fractions or anything you don't understand. Now I do because she does them again with you and shows you. Well, the teacher at the comprehensive might say 'well, you've heard me. Think it out of yourself. Sit down and carry on'.

The sense of dependence on the teacher is not so much as a conveyor of information as an explainer of *how* to go about work. When children talk about the curriculum they appreciate the work which seems to them active and engaging. They make a clear distinction between lessons where they are able to work by themselves in an experimental fashion and what they dismiss as 'writing'. One of the elements of the secondary school to which children look forward is the chance to do 'science' in a laboratory, with interesting experiments. What children do not like is 'doing the same things over and over again' or reading 'the same book so many times'. Interesting topics seem to the children to consist of activities, 'because you have to do things, like washing and cleaning and experiments'. Against this they feel that 'finding the answers is boring'. The sense of the *skills* of learning is clearly important to them.

Children are not afraid of having demands made on them. 'Easy' work is work they can understand. Once they know how to go about something they recognize the pleasure of doing so.

Girl: I like solving problems. You've got to think and work it out.

Boy: I like solving problems. Problem maths. You've got to use you brain and think and when it comes to problems I like working them out. I think the way you do things helps you to like it.

Children's pleasure in work derives from those moments when they understand the teacher's explanations and the task. The teacher is not just a responsive friendly person, but someone who is supposed to make their tasks interesting. Against the pleasure of doing work, like solving problems, children remember the many occasions when the work is undemanding, repetitive or obscure, so that they don't know *how* to go about it. there are many circumstances when children feel at a loss; not only when the teacher has not been clear, but when they feel held back by the lack of resources.

Boy: When I was in the infants we had the Ladybird books. By the second year I'd finished every single infant book they had so I had to go to the lower juniors. When I was in the lower juniors I finished all the books there so I had to get them from the upper juniors. In the upper juniors I nearly ran out of books. Because there was such a restricted thing and I found I was going ahead of everybody else.

The bright child might b able to use the circumstances better, but this is often because he is not making too many demands. The child who does stand out can be difficult to contain within the usual practices of the classroom. Often the work of school seems to children to consist of nothing but routine.

Girl:I get fed up with English sometimes because we do English exercises and they are mostly all the same because they give you a paragraph of writing and you have to answer questions on it and we do that twice a week and it just becomes a bit boring. If they gave you a paragraph and if they asked you questions about it, then if they let you write it in your own words, kind of things would be better because at the moment you have to write it the same as it is for in the paragraph.

Children are demanding clients. they want all the work geared to their individual needs, and yet derive security from being in the class, working together. They assume that the teacher will know the answers to questions and yet give them the means to find them out for themselves. They want to work to the teacher's formula and attain help from the teacher and yet learn a great deal from each other. They *all* say that they like to work with a friend for their mutual benefit. They all expect the teacher to be fair and to know what is going on in the social tensions of their own peer group. they expect the teacher to be responsive, and yet see her as a distant authority. Most difficult of all, children, in discussing the problems of school, say that the most important question is the friendliness or the distance of the teacher. And yet they also respect the most those teachers who seem to be most distant, most authoritative, and most associated with expertise in a particular subject.

All this put primary teachers in an ambiguous position. children see the complexity of their role. It is as if the attitudes towards primary schools generally prevalent in society were already being engendered in the children before they leave. they already see the secondary school as more 'important'; not only because of the examination system, and the assumption that schools are there to prepare them for jobs, but because the teachers are experts within their own classrooms, on particular areas of the curriculum. The very ability of primary school teachers to create a harmonious working atmosphere, and to deal with a variety of different subjects, is both admired by the children and seen as only a stage towards the real work they will be undertaking later, The one aspect of the role of the primary teacher that children never quite forget, is the individual attention, explanation and concern. That is something children say they miss in the secondary school. But they are also quick to adapt. So they also associate the very virtues of the primary school with a way of life they later dismiss as belonging to the more comfortable years when they were young.

9 Teachers for an Enabling Curriculum

There can be no curriculum without teachers. Indeed, Alexander claims that the primary curriculum cannot be considered apart from primary teachers. Certainly, an enabling curriculum is bound to require a distinctive approach from teachers: not necessarily greater demands, but a willingness to think in terms of the development and experience of individual children,to plan curriculum as intervention, and to consider equipping children for choice and for acceptance.

It is not only necessary for teachers to consider curriculum in the light of children's development and experience. They have also to take account of their own development and experience. They too are on a series of curves of development, physical, intellectual and social/emotional, which powerfully affect their own powers and procedure. Inevitably, different teachers are at different points on those curves. Even in primary schools the youngest teachers are nearer in chronological age to their youngest pupils than they are to their oldest colleagues. In the extreme case they may be at the pinnacle of achievement in a sport which is only a memory and a clutch of trophies to their colleague in the next classroom. In intellectual terms the younger staff may retain a flexibility of mind that acts as a counterpoint to the accumulated wisdom of the older staff. In personal terms heads nearing the end of their careers may well think of the youngest staff as, professionally, their children or even their grandchildren. Their own sons and daughters may well be considerably older than their youngest colleagues.

Quite apart from these age-differences, individual teachers change as time passes. Their patterns of relationships with colleagues and children undergo modifications as they become less physically vigorous but more generally mature, and it requires regular vigilance to ensure that an individual teacher remains aware of these changes and of their consequences. Through consistent cultivation of awareness of their own development, they become more sensitive to developmental considerations among children.

It is equally important for teachers to appreciate the significance of their own experience. In one sense this is always recognized: there is general respect for 'experienced' teachers both in selection for posts of responsibility and in recruitment for teacher education. At the same time there is widespread suspicion about teachers' lack of experience of life in general. In considering an enabling curriculum, teachers need to be aware of both these characteristics, and also to build on their experience of children to extend their own understanding of development and experience in children. In fact, any teacher gains in experience simply by dint of working with children, and gains in quality of experience by reacting sensitively to the development and experience of children. The appraisal and assessment of pupils, one activity which will shortly be discussed, is a process which becomes both easier and more accurate because it has been done before, though at the same time there is a risk that the teacher, either through personal development or experience, may alter the norm of assessment without being aware of doing so. Also, with the passage of time, there may be real differences between, say, 6-year-olds in 1980) and 6-year-olds in 1985. The difficult point to grasp and to bear regularly in mind is that the entire teaching-learning complex—pupils, teachers, curriculum, and cultural context—is changing all the time. None of us can stop the world.

There is another form of experience that has also to be borne in mind. Professional training was a very different matter when the older teachers were in college. The sequence of professional experience that, in England and Wales, leads from an Ordinary BEd. or an Open University degree to an Honours degree, or a Diploma, and then perhaps an MEd., or from a degree and Post-graduate Certificate in Education (PGCE) on to the same path, is very different from the two-or three-year Certificate course which was formerly considered adequate and self-contained, requiring only occasional supplementation with a refresher course or two as - in a significant phrase -'post-experience' training. To teachers from the more recent patterns of training, the expectation of professional growth is much more in-built.

Thus, teachers at different points on their curves of development will not only have different extents and kinds of experience. They are likely also to be differently equipped to understand and take account of the development and experience of children. This is bound to affect their general readiness to consider curriculum as planned intervention in the interaction between development and experience, though many individuals in both patterns of professional training will stand out as exceptions.

When we think of how teachers as a whole figure in relation to an enabling curriculum, a number of considerations present themselves. Some of the most prominent are these:

Are some teachers more suited than others to develop an enabling curriculum?

What kinds of equipment do teachers need in order to develop it?

What changes in teachers' role are implied if it is to be developed?

What co-operation can teachers look for among adults in developing it?

And in a different vein:

What are the implications for the initial and in-service education of teachers if an enabling curriculum is to be developed?

In the remainder of this chapter with particular reference to primary teachers in England and Wales, these issues will be examined in turn.

The first issue is as complex as it is important, and the literature relevant to it is immense. For a long time it was thought that research might reveal which people were likely to become good teachers of any kind, until it became evident that they were many kinds of person, and no simple definition of good teaching, even though it is fairly easy to recognise at least some forms of bad teaching. More recently, attention has come to be focused on particular styles of teaching or particular principles of procedure, and also on the social origins and experience of particular teachers and their congruence with particular categories of children. To take this last point first, there is some reason to think that the most appropriate teacher to understand and enable working class children, or rural children, would be a teacher from their own background; and similarly for other situations. In fact, there is little consistent evidence to that effect.

Similar considerations apply to the processes of pedagogy. These are skills that can be taught and learned in teacher education, as Stones has advocated. They are related to individual acts of teaching and learning that can figure in any structure of curriculum, and can improve teaching within it. This being so, they are important in any teacher education, including preparation for an enabling curriculum. But they are not strictly linked to that curriculum.

If neither social origins nor pedagogic skill is directly associated with suitability to enact an enabling curriculum, might it at least be true that some teaching styles are more appropriate than others for this purpose? The two principal studies of infant schools in England do not show a consistent pattern of evidence on this theme, though they do indicate its potential importance. Bennett's study was of course directly focused on teaching styles, this time in junior schools, and in the interaction between variables analysed in his study there was a distinct advance in knowledge about the effect of a range of teaching styles. However, the main dependent variable was an objective measurement of attainment, which is rather a different matter from the implementation of a particular pattern of curriculum. The Oracle team at Leicester carried this type of analysis a stage further, bringing out the interactions between styles of teaching and styles of learning, but here too the measure selected was attainment. The most directly relevant findings of the Oracle studies in relation to an enabling curriculum were probably those concerning the outcomes of class teaching. For it was demonstrated that the class-teaching pattern allowed more direct pupil-teacher interaction than was possible through 'individual monitoring' of pupils working on their own, so that, paradoxically, a curriculum that aims to cater for individual needs may do so more effectively when some teaching, particularly of subject-areas depending on sequential skill and concept formation, is done collectively. This is not to be taken as an inflexible paradigm across the curriculum. In the *Oracle* studies particular attention was paid to language and mathematical and scientific skills, and it could well be that a combination of individual and group study would be more suitable for some topic work in the social subjects. Again, there is probably a legitimate contrast between the teaching of skills in art and craft and of those required in music. In addition, any individual teacher is likely to find a particular mix of styles most appropriate for himself or herself. The criterion of appropriateness here may be more than measurable efficiency, for it could be maintained, for example, that the social experience derived from group work, suitably and sensitively handled, is more important than any outcome measured in terms of performance alone.

It is possible here only to hint at some of the implications of Bennett's studies and the Oracle publications for an enabling curriculum in primary education: and to emphasise the point that they have both made, namely, that these issues are more complex than protagonists of either 'traditional' or 'progressive' opinions have always allowed.

In general terms, then, it appears that the social origins of teachers and their actual pedagogic acts are not directly associated with any particular approach to curriculum. Teaching styles may have some relevance, though it is more a question of finding the right mix than of opting for any one style.

There still remains the possibility that teachers' personalities, motivations, characters or values might have a direct relationship with the development of an enabling curriculum. It is still more difficult to appeal to research findings for this purpose. Ashton's study of aims in primary education provides a baseline for any such investigation, but its main thrust is the relationship between particular categories of teacher, values and emphases in curriculum and other variables. If anything, it would indicate that teachers who are younger and equipped with a more sophisticated professional preparation would be likely to look more favourably on a process approach. Bassey's survey within one county portrays graphically what teachers in primary schools actually do, but does not penetrate beyond this. Neither of these studies would claim to indicate more than trends to which there are many exceptions, or to postulate that opinion as measured at the time of their studies is not liable to alteration. Indeed Ashton has explicitly pointed out what changes may be taking place Beyond this it would probably be legitimate to say that teachers with authoritarian tendencies, or with a penchant for hierarchical organisation, for dogmatic statements and enforced compliance, would not be well suited to implement an enabling curriculum; but then they would not want to. Difficulties would arise only if somebody else, applying their own methods to a different value-position, said that they had to. Such a situation is not unknown in primary education, and indeed it may be worsened if it results from an innovation introduced brusquely and without adequate consultation. For the real necessity in the development of an enabling curriculum is the commitment of the teachers concerned to a value-system consonant with its implications. In most other respects the qualities, that make good teachers in a forms-of-understanding approach or a social-imperatives approach are likely to make good teachers in a process approach. In teaching styles there may be some differences. In values and commitment, the difference is crucial. On the assumption that suitable teachers are available in suitable numbers, it is next necessary to consider what kinds of equipment they need in order to implement an enabling curriculum. For this purpose it may be useful to look at the five elements in the armour of primary teachers designated in the report of postgraduate certificate courses for teachers in primary and middle schools. They apply to primary teachers irrespective of their pattern of training. The first of these is what may be broadly described as 'technique', that is, the indispensable skills of classroom organisation and procedure. The next two require more specific comment.

One of these is curricular knowledge, including knowledge about the concept of curriculum as discussed, but also sufficient knowledge of an appropriate kind about the main components of any curriculum, including those discussed they apply to an enabling curriculum. The sheer quality of expertise that is potentially required for one teacher to mediate the curriculum discussed in those chapters is daunting, and must in practice result, at least in the upper primary years, in some form of sharing of function, Even so, a team of teachers can only just manage to cover the range of expertise in skills and familiarisation that is necessary. It must be noted that this is not a range of knowledge, for a process approach does not basically require the transfer of knowledge from teachers to children. What is required is a way of transmitting skills and concepts and attitudes. There are procedures appropriate to mathematics, to science, to art, to PE and to each other aspect of curriculum, and these are not mere concessions to the forms-of-understanding approach. The sharpening of perceptions itself depends on disciplined observation and deduction. No enthusiasm for discovery will in itself lead a teacher for example to recognise the relationship between rock type, soil and vegetation, or to place a local building in the social totality of its historic period, or to know how to evaluate the quality of significance of a child's artistic or musical invention. And if the teacher is unaware, then the quality of the curricular experience for the child is thereby diminished. It would be unrealistic to imagine that any but the most exceptional of teachers can do other than accumulate, through their own experience, some equipment of this kind and to share it with colleagues, learning meanwhile from them and from others.

Alongside curricular knowledge must be reckoned professional knowledge. This is the necessary cornerstone of an enabling curriculum, for it is through professional knowledge that a teacher is able to analyse development, experience, and their relation to curriculum. It involves familiarisation with the kinds of thinking discussed in the preceding chapters as well as with other approaches to the understanding of children in schools. It also means rather more than that, for it implies a readiness to practise curriculum design and implementation with development and experience in mind. Since each child's development and experience is unique, it might seem at first sight logically necessary to design a special curriculum for each child as planned intervention in his particular development and experience, and to keep doing so as he and his experience continue to change. Plainly, that would be absurd; yet the only practicable alternative is to enact some kind of compromise which is reasonably on-target for a class, and then to monitor each individual's progress through the common experience. It is in fact justifiable to do this, since one facet of an enabling curriculum is that it shall have common features and enable children to grow up and live together. This compromise has then to be negotiated with a class in order to secure their continuing engagement at a reasonable level, a procedure that implies not surrender but constructive realism.

If a teacher has an idea about the development and experience of a child, or the children living together in class, this implies also some notion about how learning takes place. It involves knowing how to assess progress in respect of curricular experience in different aspects of curriculum, and how to diagnose, in the process, what children are capable of doing next. This is a procedure often to be identified in practice, ranging from the infant teacher's Why don't you make me a big one, and don't forget his ears?" to the suggestion made to children in a junior or middle school: 'You two go over there and try it again, and weight what is left over'. In a broad sense each new venture is then assessed in its turn, and eventually it becomes possible to build up a cumulative record such as Clift. Weiner and Wilson advocate. In each individual learning episode this requires sensitivity about the whole process, including awareness that in each child, in each aspect of the curriculum, the profiles both of performance and of engagement are likely to be irregular, and the relation between performance and engagement, unpredictable. The skill needed to achieve this degree of sensitivity and awareness requires not only a grasp of the ways in which learning actually takes place, but a readiness to match the assessment to the learning. This is more straightforward to undertake in the sequential, skill-based aspects of curriculum, such as mathematical understanding, than in those whose structure is more open and problematical.

The remaining two elements in a primary

teacher's equipment are of a more personal nature. One is in fact the set of personal and interpersonal skills and qualities that are needed in a teacher when relating to children and indeed to other adults too. These skills and qualities include sensitive facility in matters such as the grouping of children, the possibilities of peer teaching, and indeed the organisational curriculum itself. Partly these arise from professional knowledge, but partly also from personality and character and from a teacher's own experience and the sustained habit of self-analysis. In the complex and varied organisation of a class for different purposes, it demands almost a form of intuition, which the ablest of teachers of young children seem to show, but which is actually built up through prolonged insight into the development and experience of children. The remaining element, hinted at in the discussion of personal qualities, is that of constant critical appraisal of oneself, one's aims, and one's context and outcome of action. Provided that it does not become discouraging on the one hand, or a form of self-indulgence on the other, criticism of this kind leads to the continuous readjustments that a truly enabling curriculum requires. Awareness of the hidden curriculum is particularly important here. The consequence of maintaining these five elements is that the role-complex of teachers becomes widened and the task itself of higher professional standing. In addition to the usual roles of instructor, classifier, socialiser etc. and the more fully elaborated analyses presented by, Musgrove and Taylor, an enabling curriculum requires at least three others. One is that of the teacher as *researcher*, as advocated by Stenhouse. By the mastery of procedures of systematic observation and recording, even in the most rudimentary way that is all that time permits, a teacher is able to combine the use of professional knowledge with the demands of interpersonal relations and the need for critical appraisal. Being research-minded does not mean putting on a metaphorical white coat and distancing oneself from children. It resembles far more the situation of the medical man whose research orientation sharpens his diagnosis and medication. Where it is possible, a whole range of new-wave techniques of observation and evaluation can be learned and applied, but it is the orientation, the attitude, that matters; that of learning from and in the teaching situation rather than taking oneself and one's knowledge and skills as an invariant datum. In one of his later papers Stenhouse linked the teacher's research role with that of the artist, thus imparting a new dimension to it.

The second additional role is that of *team member*. This is an almost inevitable consequence of the expansion of curricular and professional knowledge. It has already become obvious that no one teacher can master all the skills, concepts and procedures that are needed in an enabling curriculum. But it there is to be sharing, it does not take place automatically. For one thing there may not be an exact match between curricular needs and teacher competences. There may be too many geographers and too few physical scientists; a gaggle of guitarist and no pianist. In that case, a team has to look for some kind of adjustment, which in effect means either dispensing with something important for the curriculum, or seeing that somebody develops and additional expertise. Readiness to take this role has not always been characteristic of primary teachers. What is more, the newly acquired expertise—or any other expertise for that matter—may be in the hands of a junior member of staff who has to learn the skill of advising much more established teachers, while they in turn have to learn the harder skill of being advised by a slip of a girl, or a young fellow not five minutes out of college, or however it may be put. Yet this is the implication of staff development of this kind. It involves a kind of *professional status-inversion.* but it is a necessary step towards the other role of curriculum consultant that is advocated for this reason in the HMI survey of 1978.

In the remainder of this chapter attention will be given to some of the ways which schools and teachers can move towards the personnel, equipment and roles required for the implementation of an enabling curriculum.

School-based innovation

First, it is necessary to mention briefly the kinds of development can take place within a school. Basically, these must be designed and implemented by the head of a school, together with a nucleus of enthusiastic colleagues who may or may not be among the senior members of staff.

This is in itself a delicate operation, for it implies that the head must exercise a dual role, that of leader and also that of innovator, He or she must be equipped for both, and confident in an ability to discharge both. And the innovation is not only a curricular innovation, but rather an innovation in organisational climate and procedures intended to facilitate a continuing series of curricular innovations which themselves have implications for the wider curriculum. It involves getting senior and junior colleagues to accept a situation in which there will be continuing demands on professional knowledge, professional skills and curricular knowledge, and the possibility of increasing and threatening conflict in values between colleagues. Almost by definition it is a situation calculated to increase rather than to decrease uncertainty. Dewey once spoke of the need to substitute security of procedure for security of belief; but this is a case where security of procedure is itself the casualty, until a new kind of procedure is substituted. In an age in which an emphasis on either development or experience is frequently blamed for every cognitive and moral defect in the body politic, a transition within a school to a new way of looking at curriculum is likely to be still more difficult. Yet without it, any serious attempt to rethink the primary curriculum in detail must be at risk. At best it will influence two or three members of staff, who will continue to support each other until one of them leaves, after which the whole process may well falter and fail. At worst, the whole process of curriculum changes may be frozen out at the start, the reason given being that it is high-sounding theoretical idea with no practical significance, whereupon everyone heaves a sigh of relief and goes on just as before.

If the school is a very small one, a different set of problems may arise. There is no doubt a considerable value in the small, familial institution, but the demands of curricular knowledge and professional knowledge fall disproportionately on small schools, and ironically it may happen that the very efforts needed in order to make an innovation effective will cause greater strains than in a larger school which i already better equipped in terms of range of expertise and personnel. In an age of declining school rolls in so many countries the small-school problem is not itself declining, even when it is held at bay by amalgamations So this small-school problem is not likely to disappear. Meanwhile, there is even more biter irony in the contrast that those countries with growing populations and greater numbers clamouring for primary education are just those which cannot yet afford to resource an enabling curriculum at all.

Of course, in this as in most other forms of innovation, case-studies of successful initiatives provide the best evidence. These can then be used to convince others. 'Show me!' is a very understandable demand, and it should be increasingly met by those who have shown themselves what can be done.

Support agencies

Even for this purpose it is necessary to provide some effective support. The twin aspect of the researcher role, that of closer observation of children and that of enterprising experiments with formal and wider curriculum, both call for professional support beyond the resources of individual schools. Fortunately, they can be supplied by different agencies. This indicates the patterns of in-service provision that are required.

The first is concerned with the refinement of professional skills. This could well be entrusted to two kinds of agency. One is the personnel skilled in this field that are to be found in Universities, Polytechnics and Colleges of Higher Education. The practical difficulty in such matters is always that of deploying the resources of time, manpower, and money in a mutually satisfactory way. At the same time there is a different problem, that of rendering outside experts and school staff mutually acceptable. There is always the danger that both 'sides', at their own stages of professional development and experience, will stereotype the other, the personnel from higher education tending to think of the school staff as context-bound and perhaps lacking in perspective, while the staff regale each other with despairing comments about the jargon-ridden approach of their counterparts, and perhaps with lurid conjectures about how they would manage the most troublesome of the 9-year-old classes. Yet this too is a phase that can be transcended by experience based on a combined approach to curricular problems, provided that both 'sides' interact regularly with the children and genuinely value the development and experience of the other.

The other potential agency is the advisory service of the local education authorities. Here too there is a role-problem, but it is rather a different one. There may still be some suspicion of those with a lack of demonstrable recent classroom experience, but it is sometimes overshadowed by the dual role of advisors, for they are also seen as inquisitors bent on facilitating accountability. Here too collective experience can fairly soon reduce suspicions, but this requires time, which is often desperately short for both partners.

In view of the long and increasingly successful partnership that has been built up between parents and teachers, it is evident that the help of parents can be drawn upon in several ways. First, their own knowledge of their children and of their neighbours' children, especially at the infant stage, is a positive asset. If they can be persuaded that a curriculum is really intended to enable their children and not to subject them to some current fad, they can play a number of valuable roles. They and their extended families can figure also as experts in particular fields. Their development and experience can also be drawn on, and in the case of the unemployed and the retired, it may help to give significance to their own lives if they are invited to contribute from their expertise, their concerns and their memories. Families can also help particularly in the informal curriculum, when resources permit, by lending a hand in the planning and execution of journeys and visits which can make a powerful impact on the experience of children. Finally, the involvement of families can have a direct outcome because it gives them dignity and significance in front of their children and their children's friends, and contributes to the organisational curriculum by presenting the school in relation to the community, and 'to the hidden curriculum by combating value-differences between home and school.

Meanwhile there is another kind of support that may be required, in curricular knowledge itself. It is the more enterprising experts in different academic disciplines who can best help here: natural scientists, historians, geographers, social scientists—as well as those devoted to different kinds of artistic activity, and also the representatives of various aspects of political, economic, social and religious life. All of these could enrich the resources available to teachers, but it is difficult indeed to effect the necessary liaison. For one thing, unless their institution has been actively involved in the education of the young there is a lack of the basic mechanisms by which the experts can be brought together with the teachers. Casual social acquitances is one possible means of contact: team games, golf, chess and bridge have all been known to play a part in establishing such links, as have common membership of churches and of political parties, or simply chats over the garden fence. There may even be some positive virtue in what is just done 'for a pal', except that for each school such opportunities are left very much to chance. Even where they are effected, there can be problems. The Schools Council Industry Project, with whose activities for younger children I have been involved, has often encountered the problem of how to persuade personnel managers and sales representatives that the style required in primary schools is rather different from their customary forms of discourse. Here again, however, there is scope for experience to bring the participants together, and possibility is should be a part of the evolving role of heads to become facilitators of the participation of other adults in schools.

All of these suggestions may, of course, seem rather Utopian in terms both of resource allocation and of social reality. It requires a Plato or an Illich to envisage a troupe of scholars, research chemists, ballet dancers, car salesmen and representatives of British Raii holding themselves in readiness for a phone call from St Mary's or Acacia Avenue, even if they did know what to do when they arrived. In any case they can be released only occasionally for such purposes, however favourably they may regard them. In addition there can be hidden conflicts, particularly where power and identity are under potential threat. An industrial enterprise is unlikely to open up its industrial relations to intrepid questioning from Sandra, aged 7, nor is a professional historian likely to welcome being asked to make a contribution to what he perceives as something perfunctorily and uncomprehendingly termed Environmental Studies. Still less is a member of a local bureaucracy likely to submit to the sort of interrogation from primary pupils that he contrives to avoid in more public situations; and if this is done, it only gives a false and cosy impression of social realities.

All of these considerations have to be borne in mind by teachers and especially head teachers as they draw on the repertoire of potential support. They in turn constitute a form of professional experience whose acquisition is a challenge, which can result in a third addition to the role-complex of primary teachers, that of *community relations facilitator*.

Alongside these developments there is a place for more systematic professional enhancement through courses for named qualifications. Open University degrees in Educational Studies are a case in point. Further, the analysis of development and of experience could figure valuably in Diploma, Phil and MEd. course, or their equivalents, which customarily include a component of more rigorous empirical study. Where Honours BEd. courses are required to involve studies in Education and one other discipline, as is often the case, this combination is particularly well suited to a case-study of a teacher's own class embarking on something new related to the student's other main discipline.

However, it would be self-defeating if every teacher were to feel it obligatory to undertake such sustained study for a named qualification. This is only one way in which collective professional experience can be enhanced, and one that should be neither belittled nor given exaggerated importance in a teacher's career profile. The principal value to a school of having on its staff one or two members who are in disciplined study of this kind is that they can, and increasingly do, act as translators of educational scholarship and research and thus as a means of bringing their colleagues more effectively into the wider discourse of the teaching profession as a whole. This too involves and process of professional experience in which they personally may be open to the same suspicions that can attach to their mentors, but which they can learn to overcome. Incidentally, there is much to be said for introducing into courses of advanced study at least some guidance in the handling of these colleague relationships, as a necessary step towards the establishment of effective curriculum planning.

At an earlier stage in the discussion it was suggested that schools in the present circumstances may manifest a situation in which the most senior members of the staff were trained in an age in which subsequent professional development was not regarded as important when compared with the virtues of experience, while the younger ones have been educated with the opposite assumption. It is this kind of situation that is caricatured in the story of the head who basked in the security of thirty years' experience, which his irreverent colleagues preferred to regard as one year's experience, repeated thirty times. This is where professional status-inversion may arise. Ironically, the more effective the programme of post-experience and advanced study, the greater the likelihood that this professional status-inversion will emerge. The course themselves should, therefore, also include some reference to coping strategies for this purpose.

Initial teacher education

In the longer run, however, the main determinant of change in schools is the pattern of initial teacher education. If the teaching profession is to be increasingly equipped with teachers capable of planning an enabling curriculum as interaction between development and experience in the lives of children which can equip them for choice and acceptance, then it follows that their courses of initial training have to prepare them for this task. There is, of course, no need and no room for such considerations to be added to an already full programme. Therefore, the existing programme has to be used, and if necessary modified, for this purpose. It is worth while to look briefly at the way in which the necessary competence in studies of development, experience and curriculum can be fostered, and to consider how far this might involve modifying the usual pattern of course.

First, unlike teachers on post-experience courses, students in initial training are all at more or less the same point in professional development, and often in the same early-adult phase of general development too. They have thus reached a point at which it becomes possible to consider their own development with a little more insight and objectivity than is usually possible during Adolf-scence, and to learn to transcend any tendency to stereotype that they may have. They have also probably been able to observe the development of relatives and friends, to read more widely, and to begin to make valid generalisations from personal experience, to be set against the background of what they read in the professional literature. At the same time, and for similar reasons, they can also formulate opinions about their own experience and that of others, and to distinguish experience from development. This capacity can be fostered by general information about child development and social background. It is quite usual to include in a course of this kind some form of Child Study, and this appears a very suitable way of focusing attention on what development and experience mean in an individual child. It can also be enriched by some study of the child's cultural context, for as Bernstein insisted, teachers must first be acquainted with this, if they are to enable children to grow toward their own culture. But a closer analysis of development and experience in relation to curriculum is also needed. This could be a separate requirement or a prescribed part of the basic exercise itself, with an obligation to consider the implications of development and experience in that child's life for his or her curriculum. It would then be interesting to match the student's interpretation of what is desirable with the actual curricular sequence encountered by the child, and to reflect on the outcome.

So far, these requirements would involve only a slight modification in what is widespread practice at least in BEd. courses: the PGCE may allow less scope, but it should not therefore be assumed that this is impossible or unimportant. Children in fiction and autobiography, carefully selected, can reveal the relationship between development, experience and curriculum vividly, and one or two seminars based on the comparison between dissimilar child careers could quite quickly bring out some of the main issues, which could be further examined through direct observation in the course of the work in schools which is likely to constitute an increasingly important part of BEd. and PGCE courses.

Finally, due emphasis could be placed on the significance of development and experience in each piece of curriculum planning in which the students take part, individually or collectively, in concert with teachers or otherwise.

Where it is possible to make some form of IT-INSET link, and thus to lay emphasis on the importance of development and experience simultaneously in the education of new and of experienced teachers, the advantages may be considerable. Attitudes in the collaborating schools may thus be changed at the time that the new teachers' attitudes are being formed, while the resources of the 'training institutions' could be more readily made available to the schools in these circumstances.

Of course, this emphasis on development and experience as major considerations and on curriculum in relation to them should not be made at the expense of other concerns. That would not be necessary. In fact, to organise much of the philosophical, psychological, sociological and curricular content of a course in this way could well result in an actual saving of time and a sense of direction in the work itself.

Research

In this chapter attention has been focused on the changes in the teacher's role that are implied in an enabling curriculum involving planned intervention in the interaction between development and experience, and on the procedures needed to bring about such changes. In the course of examining these changes in the teacher's role, the need for a 'research' orientation was emphasised, but this was described as an attitude rather than a technical activity. In conclusion, however, it must be emphasised that there is an important, even an essential, place for specific and rigorous research to expose and extend the implications of the approach to curriculum suggested here. For example:

(1) There could be longitudinal case-studies of the responses of individual classes and of individual children to curriculum in the light of development and experience. These would

be difficult enough to conceptualise, still more to conduct, but without them the whole argument must remain to some extent speculative.

(2) There could be other studies of children's experience, by a variety of means: observation, interview, projection and other ethnographic techniques. These might be sensitively extended to an examination of the meaning of children's experience to themselves. We have much still to learn about development; but we probably have more still to learn about experience.

(3) There is much scope for studies of methods of pupil assessment appropriate to this approach to curriculum, and in particular those methods which relate to the aesthetic aspects of the curriculum and to the understanding of the natural and social word.

These are only a few of the fields which could be effectively investigated. What brings these together is that all of them can, technically, be carried out by a teacher with appropriate training and skills and interest in the course of working in a primary school. Some indication of these possibilities has already been mentioned in connection with diploma and higher-degree work, and it is increasingly recognised that among primary teachers, including infant teachers, there are a number who show in their previous studies that they have the ability to undertake work of this kind without detriment to their basic teaching role. This is as it should be. In any profession research should be substantially in the hands of the practitioners. In that way the role of research is itself more effectively maintained. For research of this kind is likely to keep to the middle road between undue subordination to instrumental needs on the one hand, and divorce from 'relevance' on the other. Research of this kind is most likely to permeat the professional consciousness and to lead eventually to the modification of practice: in this case, to the further modification of the teacher's role. Indeed, through exercise of critical appraisal, research might intervene in the interaction between their own continuing development and experience and lead them in the light of their own basic values to amend, transcend or reject the concept of an enabling curriculum itself. They would then, and only then, be entitled to do so. In which case, being entitled, they should not hesitate to do so.

10 Children's Response to the Primary Curriculum

In any discussion about curriculum, especially a curriculum with claims to be an enabling curriculum, it is important to appreciate the way that the curriculum appears to children themselves. To say that a curriculum is child-centred may mean little more than that the teacher assumes that it is right for the children. It is even possible that they may go through the motions of co-operation in developing curriculum for the sake of earning an easy life through pleasing the teacher, or even through bored tolerance. And when a teacher says 'We are all interested in frog spawn this year', the reality may be that the teacher has become interested in frog spawn and that her infectious enthusiasm has spilled over effectively on to her class.

Even if it means more than that, it has to be remembered that no topic is likely to lie at the centre of the interests of every single child in a class of thirty or more. Wilson has teased out particularly clearly the complexity of the relationship between children's interests and any definable curriculum.

To pursue this point a little further, it is necessary to think again of the relation of development, experience and curriculum as already considered. Curriculum is seen as planned intervention in the interaction of development with experience. Since every child's interaction is unique, it must therefore follow that *every child's curriculum is unique, and that in a sense every child constructs his or her own curriculum*. This is of course implicit in what has already been said about the self-curriculum, but the idea is worth pursuing further.

Previous chapters have treated the curriculum as though it was a unitary affair, made available as a package to at least a class and perhaps more. National curricula are of course made available to more than one class, to more than one school, in fact to a whole people. Yet whether the formal and wider curricula are devised for a class, a school or a people, and whatever variations they permit, still each individual constructs his or her own version of curriculum, and in the process evolves his or her own achieved version of the pupil's role. And these personal curricula differ from each other in a number of ways. The most obvious of these is *performance*, which depends quite substantially on development and experience as well as on the curriculum itself. Almost equally important is what may be called *engagement*, the extent to which children are motivated or enthused or bothered by curriculum.

There is a distinction between these two. As the *Oracle* studies remind us some good performers are able to maintain their output without giving much of themselves or, in the present terms, engaging enthusiastically with the curriculum. On the other hand, some children who engage vigorously with the curriculum simply do not perform well, like those adults who profess to like a subject while being hopeless at it. If this distinction is accepted, then a further point can be made. For if every individual child makes his or her own curriculum, then it is engagement as well as performance that is its true indication. In a curriculum with a process basis, one that emphasises skills and concepts rather than performance outputs, it becomes more defensible to emphasise the importance of engagement. At first this may seem like saying that it is better to travel hopefully than to arrive, and if a forced choice has to be made, then it is better to travel hopefully, though everyone has to arrive somewhere too, and then to move on, and on again. More important for the present discussion is the close relationship that exists between engagement and experience. To put it directly, engagement is likely to be greater where experience is more closely aligned with the formal and wider curricula of a school. That became evident. It is now necessary to look at some of the same issues in the light of performance and engagement as they relate to the continuity of children's experience throughout primary education.

Evidence of children's own 'view of the curriculum' may be taken from three sources:

descriptive writing about or for children, direct observations of children, and the results of empirical investigations that appear to throw some light on the question.

The last of these categories, the outcome of empirical studies, does not in fact help very much. There has been quite a long record of investigations into the relative popularity of school subjects at the primary stage, but this kind of study does not reveal anything more informative about the actual nature of the work that proved popular, or about the relation of preference choices to either performance or engagement. It seems at first sight likely that the relation with engagement would be closer than that with performance, but there is little evidence on this. More could perhaps be inferred from a close and continuous case-study such as those by Nash or Armstrong, but this particular question has not usually figured in such studies.

There is a wealth of information hidden in the memories of teachers, and tersely transcribed on record cards, which does show something of the relationship between performance and engagement. However, the categories are generally poorly defined, and in any case are not specifically considered in relation to experience. There is plenty of scope for something more systematic, as will be indicated, but at present the data are scanty.

Direct observation is scarcely less systematic than this. In the course of clarifying some of the ideas presented in this book, I have made a practice of checking ideas as they emerge against real children in various situations, and I hope that this precaution has in general held me back from making rash generalisations. Incidental observations of this sort can rank as evidence only in a negative, preventive sense, and it is in this way that they will be used.

There is also a third kind of evidence, a kind less usually found in what rate as professional writing about education. It includes autobiographies with vivid chapter about childhood; fictional accounts of childhood written for adults; and fictional accounts of childhood written for children by adults who have a talent for communicating with children. A whole volume could be written about the curriculum as it appears in these three kinds of writing, but that would require a particular kind of expertise and knowledge. However, there is clearly some value in taking the insights from such writing as a means of illuminating our understanding of children's perceptions, even if it is offset by the emphasis necessarily given to an author's own value, interests and preoccupations, and in particular to children's response to their own medium, the written word. So this kind of evidence will be sparingly used, as illustration here and there.

It is now possible to try to erect some form of picture of how the majority of young people respond to the formal and wider curriculum, and to suggest what implications this response may have for an enabling curriculum of the kind discussed in the previous chapters.

The minorities among children will be considered afterwards.

The formal curriculum

Most children take their formal curriculum for granted, at least at the primary level. Development impels them to envisage primary education as an accepted process in which they are taking part, the process of being at school as part of growing up. Experience embodies their reaction. Necessarily, they think of the curriculum as being first and foremost the formal curriculum, within which they usually have little doubt about the importance of the basic skills and modes of communicating. For the rest, they are likely to envisage the curriculum in terms of subject titles rather than of topics or activities, though topics and activities themselves may come to be regarded as another kind of subject: 'We did a project about that'. It is scarcely necessary to say that the enthusiasm of children for their work has little conscious relation to the curriculum theory on which it is based. Like their parents, children usually adopt quite a conventional view. They will respond to curriculum as it is, or as it changes, only if it seems in some way advantage to do so. Fortunately of enthusiastic teachers, they do usually think it advantageous to work along with somebody who is vigorous and good fun and doesn't expect the impossible. Only years later will they be able to judge how enabling their curriculum has been.

The significance of this can be taken a step further. Children themselves see some of the curriculum in terms of their growing powers: this was noted in the discussion of growth, health and movement, and it clearly applies also to the basic skills and to others such as handling a microcomputer. Much of the rest of the curriculum, however, is perceived throughout the primary years as a series of episodes to be lived through with good-humoured tolerance and with varying degrees of engagement, rather than as a series of skills, concepts and attitudes to be acquired. They are in a sense the passengers in the aircraft. Only the pilot, the teacher, has to master the route plan and the controls. The figure of speech is not quite appropriate, because now and again some of them do glimpse something of the purpose of it all, and it is an aim of primary education that they should gradually come to perceive that purpose and gain access, so to speak, to their own flight deck, as they learn to construct their self-curriculum.

Meanwhile, the formal curriculum is likely to make differing impacts on differing groups of children. This is where the question of engagement becomes important. For most children, for most of the time, the quality of engagement is not particularly high. Sometimes there is a burst of concentrated effort, especially among the younger children, but when social relations develop more richly as the children grown older, the social world of the classroom acts as a distractor to all but the most single-minded and the most socially neglected children. At the same time they may develop an effective skill in peer teaching, helping their friends either in official or in illicit ways. Indeed, one way of justifying ability and effort, and thus of avoiding ostracism, is to pass one one's knowledge and skill unconditionally, thereby frustrating any competitive ethos that may be officially encouraged. Teachers who prefer a co-operative ethos can here work with the grain, but have to remember that as soon as this co-operation becomes official policy, the social situation is changed. As a safety-valve, there must still be forms of co-operation that are officially discouraged but unofficially tolerated; and that then becomes a part of the organisational and hidden curricula. And needless to say there are other children in whose case it is a minor triumph for a teacher to persuade them to engage in any effort at all, even though they have considerable ability that occasionally shines through their protective armour. A case in point is that of Gowie Corby in Gene Kemp's tale of Cricklepit Combined school, *Gowie Corby Plays Chicken:*

The morning is long and draggy and boring.

I get half my maths wrong and have to do it again, and Miss Plum tears a page out of my English book 'cost it's so untidy, and I just can't be bothered to turn on my Tom smile. The radio programme we have on Thursdays must have been written by morons with the most awful snobby accents you've ever heard, and I get told off for drawing swastika over my pamphlet.

The realism may be slightly overdone, but it is a healthy reminder of the element of negotiation that always has to intervene between teachers and children in the real world. As Jackson points out in his memorable analysis, it is by no means necessarily the case that high motivation correlates with high performance. The recent increase of interest in classroom interaction studies betokens a willingness to concentrate on this process of negotiation. At first it may appear synonymous with capitulation on a teacher's part, a point that will be discussed further. But in fact it is a recognition of a reality that is, and must be, characteristic of all effective education, and is itself of the society that they learn to understand. The actual way in which time is spent in a classroom or a playing field or a gymnasium is bound to involve co-operation and consent by the children as well as authority one the part of the teacher. That consent may be given grudgingly, willing or in sheer terror. But it has to be given. The task of the teacher is then that of ensuring that the terms of the treaty are such as to maximise the learning opportunities of the class as a whole, as the teacher sees them. But those opportunities will never reach 100 per cent, even if some theories of curriculum seem to implify that they might.

This being so, the formal curriculum negotiated with one child will involve more engagement than the formal curriculum negotiated with another child. Within the experience of any one child the negotiated curriculum will involve more engagement on one day than on another, and perhaps more in one year than in another. So each child has a profile of engagement which may, or may not, be closely associated with performance. For now, the important consideration is how this related to the totality of experience.

On this question some clues may be drawn from retrospective comments frequently made by adults. Often these refer to specific incidents within the formal curriculum, as would be expected form the essentially concrete and episodic character of children's experience. A visit from an unusual adult, or more often a school trip to a centre such as London or York or their equivalents elsewhere, is often remembered, sometimes with a mixture of awareness of the medieval past with sing-songs in the coach on the way back. Sometimes, it must be admitted, a teacher's mistake is remembered better than a string of successes: the day when a science experiment went wrong, or when a load of coke was delivered during a hushed pause in a music broadcast. There is no easy way of telling whether the eventually learning suffered at all by reason of such disjunctions. A touch of the slapstick humour beloved of young children, however unintended, may in fact help.

By way of contrast with these examples of disengagement and of casual encounter, there are instances of intense curricular impact on individual children, answering some powerful interaction between development and experience in their own lives. This is another topic on which the evidence from literature throws light. In Jane Gardam's *A Long Way from Verona* one girl's poetic talent is persistently nurtured through episodes ranging from the absurd to the tragic with the formal English curriculum playing a not insignificant part. And in the astonishing autobiography of Helen Forester, set out in her two volumes *Twopence to Cross the Mersey* and *Liverpool Lass*, The feeling for language and literature first developed in a sheltered primary curriculum eventually survived an adolescence of incredible adversity, and, literally, enabled her to tell the tale. In her case it remained the one sustaining experience when development was soured and when home and environment failed: single-minded engagement leading to performance. It is understandably rarer to find similar examples embodied in literature of children for whom science or technology has proved to be the significant curricular element, through there are instances enough in which history or geography or the arts have exercised an appeal, sensitively, right from the earliest years. A public climate in which such commitment is ridiculed does not succeed in extinguishing it, but it does cause small agonies which are not revealed in studies of the sociology of the curriculum.

The wider curriculum

Children's response to the wider curriculum is at least as important. Indeed, they may regard the formal curriculum as a rather tiresome intrusion in the experience which is the wider curriculum. To some the informal curriculum is where they come into their own. They are the stars of the teams and of the plays and clubs, the ones who stay behind after school and get to know the teachers in a more direct way, and it is incidents in the informal curriculum that they remember most vividly. They may include some who also shine in the formal curriculum, but the informal aspects are what appeal most to them, the ones within which their social relationships are forged. They have a particular developmental significance too, because these are so palpably matters appropriate for children of their age, with an evident potential for leading towards the next step. These are the activities in which their elder sister once excelled,that sister whose current preoccupation with her boyfriend is now made the subject of a mixture of mockery and awe, or in which their elder brother first learned to take the measure of school long before he became devoted to his motor-bike and his mates. There is, in fact, a wider range of engagement in the informal curriculum, with consequences for the kind of performance that is found, according to the ways in which informal activities are perceived.

Activities within the informal curriculum attract considerable attention in literary material. They range from those to whom it included elements of agony, as in Betjeman's *summoned by Bells,* to those to whom it is a consuming passion. What is shared by the two extremes is a sense of the vividness and importance of informal activities, and in any enabling curriculum they must surely be prominent. For some children, indeed, they may provide the one moment of significance in primary education.

Closely associated with the informal curriculum is the organisational curriculum, the messages conveyed by the school as a social organisation. Usually it is seen as a centrally important matter. Its 'taken-for-granted' nature seems accepted even by truants, and in works of fiction it is usually portrayed as something to be 'sent up' and treated with light-hearted and tolerant confidence when all is going well; as a menace when there is an important test or when it is time for transfer form one stage to the next; as an intrusive nuisance in moments of high drama within the children's social world; but as a very present help in times of real trouble or terror, when even the toughest surprise themselves and everyone else by crying too. The reliable world of rules and orders is then seen to have its point, as is shown, for example, in Bernard Ashley's *Terry on the Fence*, written by an understanding author drawing on his own experience as a headmaster.

It is not just the order but the values of the school, the hidden curriculum, that are involved here. Sometimes it may engender opposition. Sometimes, however, it may express a deep concern for individuals and exemplify genuine social education in action. For example, in Tom Wakefield's *Forties Child* the author, recalling his wartime childhood, singles out the cuddling and comforting of a particularly revolting classmate by the teacher, and the challenge to accept the girl, smell and running nose and all, that the teacher directed to the author himself: 'I suppose Miss Craddock made us all a bit older—or something like that'.

On the other hand, a latent attitude of racial prejudice can engender fierce resentment among children, though here it is necessary to remember that the prejudice may not lie entirely, or even mainly, with the teacher.

Similar issues are, of course, raised when religious or class or gender differences are involved. It is scarcely necessary to say how important they can be in influencing individual children in the extent and nature of their engagement with the curriculum. To cite instances of literature that deal with any of these aspects of the hidden curriculum would be hazardous, since there are so many of them. But this in itself emphasises something of the widespread recognition of the importance of these issues. Here again, no enabling curriculum can be adequate unless it takes them sensitively into account.

It was emphasised that children's experience, even their experience in school, is not confined to the formal and wider curriculum. There is always a part of experience that exists alongside the curriculum, and one of the latent functions of primary education is that it provides an arena within which this experience can be enacted. One of the perennial messages from school stories over the past hundred years is that the secret life of children is powerfully influential in their experience and in interaction with their development. Here, more than within the curriculum, are concentrated the episodes which arouse their attention, their effort, their excitement and anger and grief. It is as if their wider experience swamps the curriculum from time to time, like flood water after a storm. This again is a common theme in literature. As the plot thickens, teachers continue woodenly to implement the curriculum, especially the formal curriculum, like some shadowy backcloth in a drama, occasionally shouting from back stage that someone is not attending, and then being fairly satisfied with an answer and fading out of experience again.

In fact, this experience beyond the curriculum can be interpreted as a collective alternative self-curriculum, for over the years it involves learning, in the neighbourhood but more intensely in the playground, a succession of codes and adjustments and conventional learned responses through which children complement their development with collective experience. It is here that pecking-orders are established and unmade, that the alleged conventional wisdom of the adult world is challenged, and that the more popular and confident individuals make their first half-ashamed, half-amused bids for heterosexual recognition.

The boundary between all this and curriculum is a real but invisible one. The ringing of a bell or the clapping of hands may be all that divides the one from the other; but every body knows where the boundary is, and everybody except the most extreme advocates of pedagogic liberty assumes that it should be, more or less, there.

This leaves unanswered the question whether the school should officially concern itself with what happens beyond that boundary. In one sense it must; there are regular appeals through the organisational curriculum when some little procession brings a casualty to the teacher. Yet despite the existence of pastoral-care systems there may be a variety of views among the children, as well as the teachers, about how vigilant those teachers ought to be, and how far it is better to let them have their own, quite false, views about what is going on. It could be that willingness of individual children to engage in curriculum is related to what happens to them outside it.

In a boarding school, or elsewhere where social relations among children are concentrated in school with particular intensity, these issues are all the more cogent. Independent primary schools include a number of boarding schools and, while term lasts, they are total institutions. That means that the wider curriculum occupies a very large part of life, but not all of it. There is still an area of autonomy within which social relations can be worked out with all the stark directness portrayed in school stories, such as Philip Toynbee's *A School in Private*.

There, as in day schools, the impact on individuals has much to do with their family and social context, and it is easy to see this as a simple, clean form of socialisation that is a part of Life. But this cannot be assumed. The seeds of disengagement with curriculum can be sown in the seedbed of non-curricular experience, for children who do not succeed in these relationships may learn to reject the whole context with which they are associated.

Minorities

Hitherto the child's-eye view of the curriculum has been confined to what happens within the normal stream of events in normal schools. It is important to emphasise this. For in a sense there is no such thing as an ordinary school, or ordinary children. However much they may try to be ordinary so as not to be left out of the swim, they are in fact all different. Of course, every respectable theory of the primary curriculum says that they are all different, but so often leads to actual curriculum planning that assumes that they are all, in most important respects, alike. The curriculum then comes to symbolise alikeness: this is what we do when we are all together and being alike, as distinct from what we do outside when we are all being different. Indeed, school itself often comes to symbolise the alikeness of society in its public guise. In a sense this is itself a valuable part of the organisational curriculum since it promotes social cohesion and security. Norms are more closely observed in the classroom. To cry, or swear, or be sick in class is on a par with such behaviour in church, though more immediately penalised. However, the limit of its value is reached at the point at which teachers slip into the habit of thinking that this classroom alikeness extends outside. As is often revealed in informal situations such as discos or school journeys, 'normal' children may turn out to be more enterprising, more aggressive, more original or more vulnerable than school suggests. The formal curriculum is thus revealed as a very special and protected kind of experience, and the enabling function of the wider curriculum is thus thrust into greater prominence.

There does, however, often come a point at which the semblance of normality cannot be maintained, even within the formal curriculum. Engagement may become so minimal that performance is seriously impaired. The children most prone to this disengagement are those with serious physical or mental handicaps. The sheer problem of managing themselves becomes significant, even when they are strongly encouraged to belittle their handicaps, and very much want to do so. This is a central problem of the social psychology of special education, one that acquires a further urgency when children with handicaps are educated alongside others, as the 1981 Education Act advises for England and Wales. Some light is thrown on this issue by autobiographical accounts. It is one that teachers are coming to recognise more generally, and it is impressive how much they can achieve, even when enabling is such an apparently formidable task, and how much it is appreciated when they do. Presumably the extreme case of enablement is that of Anne Sullivan's handling of Helen Keller's multiple handicaps and their social consequence: but that was not in school.

It is not easy to know how the least able children perceive the curriculum, except by inference, since they are the ones who find most difficulty in articulating their problems and are thus doubly disadvantaged. It seems likely that a personal, dependent, relationship with the teacher will be more prominent than any particular aspect of curriculum, and that therefore there is a form of engagement that can facilitate performance. Here too there is a dilemma, because the satisfaction of group membership, always rather fragile for the less bale, is sometimes difficult to reconcile with the need for some element of segregation so that the teacher can make the formal aspects of an enabling curriculum more personally relevant.

The case of the emotionally disturbed children is still more difficult. Here the barrier to engagement lies precisely in the area of personal relationships. There may be some unfortunate element in the interaction of development with experience that renders curriculum as such, relatively impotent, and that also leaves the teacher encumbered with the problem of first coming to terms with this. Severe case are of course allocated to special institutional contexts, but the facilities simply do not exist for all emotionally disturbed children to be transferred from 'normal' schools, especially when it is considered more important that they should not be taken away from other children than that they should be in the hands of specially trained teachers able, for example, to use the aesthetic aspect of curriculum diagnostically and therapeutically.

In all these instances of children with special educational needs, their own perceptions of what curriculum is about will be heavily dependent on those special needs. At the worst it may be beyond a teacher's powers to devise for them the special curriculum that they can make their own. At the best, the need to do exactly that for them may encourage teachers to do likewise for all their pupils; but that requires outstanding quality.

There is another category of children whose perceptions of curriculum in all its aspects are now becoming a matter of concern. These are the children from minority groups. Whose entire ambience in experience can dominant their pattern of engagement and thus, to a large extent, their performance also. Particular problems arise with children from strict and unusual family back-grounds who find a school's moves to lax and unstructured for their experience, or for those from permissive or structureless homes who regard school discipline with incredulity. Both set a real problem for the moral curriculum. In some sense their situation is not unlike that of the children with special educational needs: often, of course, they overlap with them.

However, the presence of ethnic minorities raises a different set of problems. The first of these, familiar to all who have worked in the field of multi-cultural education, is the danger of lumping all such groups together in a general stereotype such as 'non-native', 'immigrant', 'non-English-speaking' and within each group as marked individual differences as within 'normal' schools, despite apparent uniformities of dress. Yet to every one of these children the curriculum has to be related to a distinctive pattern of development and experience. Some ethnic groups do in fact show different average patterns of physical and social development when compared with the native children. All of them draw on different backgrounds of experience within which the concept of curriculum will itself occupy very different positions. For example, a Hong Kong Chinese family running a restaurant has clear expectations for, and from, its children in a way that a West Indian family headed by a unemployed second-generation immigrant may not. A whole study could be based on the different ways in which each group might envisage each of the six elements in the formal curriculum discussed, not to mention the three aspects of the wider curriculum. Moreover, any such conjecture, however true of the 'normal' members of these groups, is likely to be wide of the mark where individuals are concerned.

Almost by definition, the aspects of the curriculum that are least familiar to all of them, and most difficult for them to engage with, are those most deeply embedded in the host culture, such as English history and English literature. Even this does not result in a uniform policy or a uniform response. From one point of view, one that is clearly represented among some of the groups concerned, the learning of such initially alien content is itself the means of acquiring acceptance and of facilitating performance. The opposite point of view is that it should be rigorously excluded, and that in its place there should be some version of Black Studies or its equivalent in other cultures. Between these two comes the 'melting pot' view, in which everyone contributes from their own culture and the sum is better than its parts. Clearly, it is not possible to follow more than one of these at once. What is less immediately clear is that to follow any of them involves substituting a social-imperatives approach for a process approach to curriculum and thereby perhaps aggravating the situation, since a social-imperatives approach draws attention to group differences, while a process approach places its empahsis on individual differences. It appears that much minority in-group opinion is in favour of a curriculum that takes account of groups consciousness as such, but then such views may come from individuals particularly prone to express them. Even if this is not the case and ethnic consciousness really is paramount in children's experience in a divided and prejudiced society, it still does not follow that the most effective curricular response is to be obtained by aligning the axis of the curriculum with that of the prejudice. In multi-cultural education many of the answers are still to be found. In finding them, the evidence from the children's patterns of engagement is still one of the most important considerations.

Similar considerations apply, though perhaps less starkly, to social class and community differences, as was indicated and also earlier in the present chapter. Much the same also characterises the children's own reactions. There is a general realisation that children do disengage from the curriculum even in the primary years. It is less certain that this disengagement is mainly on account of social-class or community differences. There are middle-class rebels and working-class aspirants, and both are likely to be articulate enough to exemplify their attitudes in writing. In almost every such case there is something in the immediate personal experience of the children or their families which proves decisive for their pattern of adjustment. Therefore, adaptation of the curriculum to ensure engagement, or for social-imperatives reasons, does not guarantee any one pattern of response. Although *Nymphs and Shepherds* are remote from the experience of many children in most environments, it is not so easy to be sure what to put in their place.

One final aspect of children's response must be remembered. The proportion of families who change house, and of children who perforce change schools, is considerable: between one-quarter and one-third, and more in some areas. For each of these there is a need for readjustment on each occasion, and sometimes there are many such occasions, for example in the case of children of members of the armed services. Any such move may entail an obligation to make a mark quickly, even brusquely, in the new community in order to assert a place in the local pecking order, or even to re-assert in after a period of absence, as Edward had to do in Penelope Lively's exquisite *Going Back:*

On our first day back they cornered Edward in the playground. 'Are you with our gang then?'

And Edward, bewildered, found himself plunged into unfamiliar arrangements of alliances and enmities. The brothers had swallowed most of the school, lock, stock and barrel: either you were with them, or you were an outcast, beyond the law, a price on your head. With difficulty, he escaped them, for that day.. I said, 'Perhaps they'll just leave you out of things.

That's what girls would do.'

'Yes.'

They didn't; and when the fight came, Edward was not disgraced. But until it came, he had little time to think much about curriculum.

When children come from sharply contrasted cultural groups which, as has been pointed out, are already in a minority position, the additional problems of horizontal transition may demand a higher price, especially when the school's formal and hidden curricula operate by means that the newcomer's own culture regards as meaningless, repressive, or simply wrong. Nevertheless, after while they usually take such experiences in their stride, and gain in social maturity by doing so. Yet in the process they may lose beliefs and qualities that are not easily restored, while their intellectual development may be more seriously retarded than many people realise. In their case the need for an enabling curriculum to intervene in the interaction between development and experience and to cultivate choice and acceptance is a very real and demanding one.

There are other children who have to spend periods of their life in hospital, or ill at home, while still others absent themselves as truants or under family pressures. Systematic studies have been made of such children and their education and these help to ensure that they remain represented in the professional culture of teachers: necessarily so, for there are some in most schools and most classes, and they remain recalcitrant exceptions to most neat schemes of curriculum planning.

Like many other issues touched upon in the present study, this could constitute a whole important field of investigation in itself. What children think about their primary education is still only imperfectly known. Studies of the relative popularity of subjects or activities, contributions to newspaper competitions, and even close observation of children and teachers interaction in classrooms, do not fill in the whole picture. Many teachers can supplement the written word from their own experience of schools and children, but even they do not plumb the whole of the pupil's perspectives; there is almost always some element of surprise when children vouchsafe their opinions more openly than in usual. There is always more to be found out about children, however well one knows them, and teachers realise this too. They may be encouraged by realising that they, as a professional group, do emerge from all of this welter of veriegated evidence in a fairly favourable light; and sometimes children think the world of them.

11 Change and the Primary School

This chapter considers just two aspects of the complex issue of social and educational change: to what extent are primary schools able to respond to external changes, and what is their capacity to change their own practices? The broader question of how far schools do, or should, initiate, influence or merely mirror social change is beyond our scope here though we should remind ourselves of the somewhat banal observation that the school-society relationship is interactive.

The competence to respond to external events and influences presupposes the ability to understand, analyse and make judgments about them. For this reasons the ideological polarisation of 'child' and 'society' can have serious practical consequences, not least in producing tendencies to resist the pre-emptive analysis which is needed and to react merely to those events and pressures which become irresistible.

As an example of the latter tendency we might consider the fate of two recent reports dealing with different areas of the curriculum.

The Cockcroft report on school mathematics

and the Gulbenkian report on the arts in Schools both made powerful cases for their respective curriculum areas in terms of both social utility and the child's educational needs. A rational observer might expect the two reports to be treated with equal seriousness: indeed, if anything, the case made for the arts as central 'core' elements of the curriculum was the more powerfully made. In fact, as might have been anticipated, not only have the reports had unequal impact at school level but many teachers appear not even to have heard of Gulbenkian. Cockeroft was commissioned by the Secretary of State; Gulbenkian by an independent foundation. Cockcroft dealt with an area of existing priority; Gulbenkian did not. Cockcroft has become the new orthodoxy for initial and in-service courses and indeed for the every professional vocabulary. By such means the 'reactive' approach to educational change tends to confirm rather than question established curriculum assumptions and priorities.

Other examples are perhaps more familiar. Individualised' and 'group' teaching instituted, apparently, with more attention to external appearances than the quality of learning; informal methods, vaguely and variously defined; the rise and fall of primary French; the uses and abuses of structural apparatus in primary mathematics; varieties of writing all bearing the label 'creative' but rarely evincing creativity; and now micro-computers in every school but for purposes as yet undefined.

This scenario, illustrating the reactive approach to change, comes about partly for reasons to do with the extent of that intellectual autonomy which we defined and explored. For, though it is true that in respect of all 'swings of the pendulum' the problem for many teachers has been partly institutional or political—pressure, real or perceived, from a head, an adviser, parents or something termed vaguely 'society'—it is also the case that such pressure was the more successful for not being counterbalanced by critical appraisal. Not all these pressures and changes were irresistible or inevitable; in many instances teachers had the freedom to reject them, but executive without intellectual autonomy is, and was shown to be, hardly autonomy at all.

We have explored some of the characteristics and causes of this situation in earlier chapters - the dominance of ideology over rationality; the appeal to individual intuition rather than empirical study or collective experience; the prevailing climate of anti-intellectualism; the narrow knowledge base of primary teaching and the failure of initial training in respect of both this and the generation of the ability to theorise; the enforcement of class teacher isolation and parochialism by the school culture and by the prevailing model of headship which removes all but day-to-day operational matters from the class teacher's shoulders; and the unremitting pressure of class teaching.

Circumstances, then—norms of professional discourse, initial training, the organisation and culture of the school—combine both to discourage a constant and critical perspective on change and to deny access to the requisite knowledge and skills. This is certainly not to say that such capabilities do not exist, but rather that the many teachers who seek and gain such a perspective do so often in the face of considerable contrary norms and constraints. Their resources are personal rather than situational, and their insistence upon swimming against the tide and valuing reading, theorising, ideas and argument can cause them acute problems in certain school settings where, perhaps. They risk the charge of 'airy-fairy' indulgence or of encroaching on the territory of the head as the school's resident and sole philosophiser.

Handling change within schools depends on comparable abilities—the teacher needs to be able to analyse situations, diagnose needs, conceptualise and appraise alternative strategies and solutions, and evaluate their implementation. The organisational and interpersonal skills of 'making things happen' are central, a *sine qua non,* but have no role without a framework of educational justification.

We shall need to bear this last point in mind as we consider now various emergent mechanisms whereby schools are being encouraged to cope with change—mandatory management courses for heads and deputy heads, the enhancement of posts of responsibility, the rehabilitation of curriculum schemes and guidelines, and the proliferation of procedures for evaluation and self-evaluation, for example. In respect of each such strategy we shall need to consider not only its practical efficacy but its conceptual and ethical basis and the kinds of intellectual as well as organisational demands it places on the teachers concerned.

The head's leadership

To say that primary heads have substantial power is not to say that all primary heads are autocratic, still less that the power is abused. It is a concomitant of the possession of power that its holders can choose to exercise it in different ways, to the point, indeed, of introducing widespread delegation and power-sharing. But it is also a function of power that the choice in this matter is the head's alone, and he has no formal obligation to account to a school's staff for the way he decides to conduct the decision making process.

Thus the pivotal point in the matter of how a school copes with change is the *leadership* provided by the head. Studies of leadership tend to use two or three 'ideal types'. Lewin's early typology—'autocratic', 'democratic', and 'laissez-faire'—has proved durable and influential, though, as Nias points out, such terms are capable of many interpretations and are rendered particularly problematic by their evaluative connotations. Thus 'automatic', in a society whose leaders constantly invoke their 'democratic' credentials, soon acquires dictatorial overtones,. Similarly, 'democratic' can sustain many different interpretations, from 'popular power in the majority interest' to 'representative democracy conditional upon open elections'. In turn both such poles have variants; witness; witness the arguments about proportional representation. So a stimulative and neutral definition of such terms is needed if they are to be useful. We also used the terms, 'instrumental' and 'expressive'. These terms can also be applied to leadership, as indeed they were by Etzioni.

Commenting on the various studies and the problems they arise, Nias suggests that quite apart from the value-connotations, such 'ideal-type' approaches have tended to be rather one-dimensional. She offers instead these three dimensions:

(a) initiating structure; the degree to which a head defines and structures his or her own role and that of his or her subordinates towards goal attainment;

(b) consideration; the degree to which a leader acts in a warm and supportive manner and shows concern and respect for his or her subordinates;

(c) decision-centralisation; the degree of leader influence over group decisions.

Where earlier 'ideal types' like 'autocratic', democratic' and 'laissez-faire' were presented as mutually exclusive, these are interdependent dimensions of leadership.

The particular way they combine produces a head's dominant leadership characteristics, and

Nias found that though, naturally, there is infinite variety in leadership styles as in all aspects of human behaviour, there was a tendency for behaviours to cluster in ways amenable to representation as three leadership 'types'. which she termed 'passive'. 'bourbon' and 'positive';

1. The 'passive' head: (a) sets a low professional standard; has a low level of personal involvement in the school; does not monitor the standard of teachers; has an inefficient administration; (b) is not easy to talk to and does not support individual teachers: (c) has no perceived aims. This type of head was not favoured by Nias's teacher respondents.
2. The 'bourbon' head :(a) has an inefficient administration; (b) treats individual teachers as inferiors; (c) does not allow participation in goal-setting or decision making. This type of head was not favoured by Nias's respondents.
3. Then 'positive' head, whom Nias's respondents preferred: (a) sets a high professional standard; has a high level of personal involvement in the school; (b) is readily available, especially for discussion; is interested in individual teachers' development, (c) gives a lead in establishing aims for the school; encourages participation in goal-setting and decision-making.

In other words, a head fan be both 'instrumental' and 'expressive': can provide firm leadership and involve staff in decision making. Indeed it is the reconciliation of the explicit exercise of power with a high degree of staff involvement and a 'caring ' climate which gains most teacher approval and seems to provide a context which permits both job satisfaction and goal achievement.

A similar point is made by Whitaker when he identifies 'concern for people' and 'concern for task' as the two central dimensions of leadership and by the use of a grid argues that the optimum position is for a head to score high on both dimensions rather than pursue tasks at the expense of people.

This juxtaposition of positive leadership and involvement is a useful antidote to the kind of argument which equates school democracy with purposeless chat or even anarchy, a sort of leaderless confusion. This characterisation is popular among 'bourbon' heads anxious to resist participation, In fact it is a characterisation not of democratic but of laissez-faire regimes.

The few people who have written analytically about primary headship tend to conclude that since something approaching Nias's 'positive' leadership both works in practice and is preferred by teachers, it provides the best basis for development. HMI in the middle school survey link the head's positive leadership, high expectations and exemplary teaching with 'higher standards'. Coulson, Nias and the Schools Council all argue, for example, for 'collegiality': the head, are accountable for the various and specific responsibilities they exercise. The head would become a chief executive, but the right single handedly to determine or dominate policy and decision making would cease.

On the face of it this may seem a sane and civilised development, but in fact transition is fraught with difficulty, attitudinal as well as procedural, and for the staff as much as the head. For while collegiality requires that a head treats the staff as 'professionals' rather than 'employees', it also necessitates that staff too see themselves as —in Hoyle's terms—'extended' rather than 'restricted' professionals, concerned with the school as a whole rather than their own classroom only. And while the kind of paternal/maternal role complementarity we explored may discourage the development of true intellectual autonomy, it could be argued that at least, after a fashion, it works. To argue that collegiality is desirable is thus to miss the point that some class teachers themselves - rather than, exclusively, the head - may prefer paternalism as long as it is reasonable and benevolent, since it absolves them of responsibilities over and above that of running their class. That this point does not emerge from Nias's study may reflect a typicality of her respondents. They were young PGCE trained graduates, whose educational background, it seems fair to assume, would tend to predispose them towards intellectualist views of teaching and school decision-making. It could also be argued that as a distinct, and privileged, minority, PGCE—trained teachers might feel this made them 'different to the point, perhaps, of tending to reject the dominant professional culture which they might perceived by other staff - whether they were or not - as stand-offish or 'superior'. Consciousness of this perception would compound the difficulty.

Three points of some importance emerge from the discussion so far. The first is that positive leadership, participation and individual autonomy are not - as they are often held to be—mutually exclusive: on the contrary, each seems to be an essential ingredient if a school is to continue to grow and to cope with changes. Second, the matter of leadership is not merely one of style, still less of mere procedures but revolves fundamentally round the question of attitudes to and perceptions of the respective roles of a head and a class teacher, and to/of the characteristics of a community of professionals. Third, that though the head's leadership is pivotal, the attitudes on such matters held by class teachers are as significant for the 'health' and effectiveness of the school as those of the head.

Apart from matters of practical strategy, which we will not neglect, such questions tend to highlight two central issues - accountability within the school, and teacher expertise.

Internal accountability: a framework

It is noted elsewhere that discussion of accountability tends to focus on extra-institutional relationships, on the 'public accountability of whole institutions to the outside bodies who have a claim to know how they are performing. In the present political climate such concern is understandable, but it rather detracts from the equally pressing matter of a school's internal accountability relations and procedures. Collegiality, participation, 'positive', 'passive' and 'bourbon' leadership all generate a fundamental question concerning the extent to, and manner, in, which head and staff should or should not be accountable to each other. Bearing in mind the Sussex project's distinction between 'moral', 'professional' and 'contractual' accountability, the answer is clear for as long as one defines accountability solely in contractual terms. The class teacher, like the head, is contractually accountable to LEA, but the class teacher accounts in the first instance to the head whereas the latter is accountable directly. Viewed in this way, therefore, accountability is straightforward and hierarchical: this, essentially is the argument invoked by heads in support of autocratic leadership.

We have established, however, that so one-dimensional a view of professional relationships is inadequate because teaching is complex and value-saturated, and happens to involve children and parents as well as employers. Acknowledging these complexities, therefore, we might consider not one mode of accountability but five.

Professional accountability within the school: five 'ideal types'

1. *Managerial*. This reflects the assumption that individual teachers are exclusively accountable to those who administer and control the school and who allocate human and other resources to their work. What goes on in their classroom,

therefore, is of legitimate concern to such 'managers' and to them alone.

2. *Consultative*: This reflects the view that, as professionals, teachers in a school hierarchy have a right to be involved in discussions about their work but that the form of such involvement and the control decisions still rests with the head. It is the version of 'democratic' decision-making operated in many educational institutions and is a familiar response at local and national government levels to pressure for public 'participation' in decision-making.

3. *Autonomous*: This reflects the assumption that what goes on in a particular school or classroom is the sole responsibility of the professional most immediately concerned. It rests on a view of individuals—whether teachers, or heads—as professionally competent over the full range of activities they undertake, and this competence includes the necessary knowledge and skills to make or seek insightful and valid appraisals of their work and to act on those appraisals. Their status as 'professional' is a guarantee of the integrity of their work. The teachers, or heads, then, are accountable chiefly to themselves.

4. *Mutual*: This reflects the view that education has to be conceived as a collective enterprise, so that all who participate directly in a particular educational activity have a legitimate interest in its quality and progress;

that such quality and progress being the result of the particular contribution which each participating individual makes, participants should account to each other for their various contributions. Being the most public and open form it is some distance from 'autonomous accountability' at the individual teacher level, though in fact it is essentially a model for professional autonomy at the whole profession level. It does not necessarily incorporate any particular structural view of school decision-making it allows for continued role and status-differentiation, such as is probably inevitable in schools. It is egalitarian only in the sense that it requires that all participants, regardless of role or status , see themselves as equally accountable to each other for their particular contributions to the educational process.

5. *Proletarian*: This is the exact reverse of managerial accountability in that the accounting relationship is downward from those given managerial responsibility to the 'workers'. At the same time it is neither an 'autonomous' model nor 'autonomous' model. This, since it implies grass-roots staff control is the least likely in the British educational context, but it is a theoretical possibility, and of course, like all the other models it has its counterpart, as a working out of the relationship of the individual to the state, in national political systems.

To summarise: 'managerial' and 'consultative' accountability assume accounting upwards only; 'proletarian' assumes downwards only; 'autonomous' denies accountability, other than contractual, to others; and 'mutual' assumes omni-directional ready comparison with situational realities explored in this book. 'Autonomous' is that privatisation most prevalent in primary classrooms and university departments. While it may not necessarily include the kind of intellectual autonomy needed to justify the extent of executive freedom claimed, it is on intellectual autonomy that the claim rests. Strict 'managerial' and its perhaps commonest variant 'consultative' accountability are the traditional models for primary headship. 'Proletarian' is there as a theoretical possibility, but rarely emerges in practice - some of the 1960s/1970s 'free schools' may be the nearest.

This leaves 'mutual' accountability. If one were to rehearse the arguments of earlier chapters it would be seen that the case for mutual accountability in primary schools is strong. Strict 'managerial' accountability can alienate staff in the way explored earlier and deskill them in terms of the kinds of cultural and educational awareness the class teacher needs. The privatisation of 'autonomous' accountability may offer the freedom which creative teaching needs, but in so extreme a form may feed the curriculum incoherence and inconsistency as between teachers and classes which emerges from recent surveys. A 'while curriculum' as we have considered it can exist only in a climate of mutuality, with openness, the sharing and comparing of ideas, and the dovetailing of schemes and practices. And if primary schools are serious in their commitment to educational goals for the child like co-operation, the development of empathy, inter-personal skills and so on, they need to acknowledge the force of the hidden curriculum in such matters whereby the behaviour of adults in the school towards each other is as significant a learning resource as, say, group work in the classroom. The espousal of curricular goals for the child of holism and social inter-dependence is not compatible with either autocratic management for teacher privatisation.

The 'ideal types' of accountability above are a framework. The required exercise for each school is to ask the following questions:

1. What accountability relationships do existing management and decision-making procedures embody?
2. Are these appropriate in the professional community?
3. Are these compatible with the school's educational goals?
4. Might alternatives be considered?

Curriculum schemes and guidelines

Both the 1978 and 1982 HMI survey link curriculum quality with a school's use of schemes and guidelines as well as with responsibility posts; indeed the former are presented as the latter's child tool. 'Schemes' were once universal in primary schools: the head presented the teachers with a set covering all or most aspects of the curriculum, and expected them to teach to its prescriptions. The weekly record-book or forecast enabled the head to monitor the teachers' adherence to the schemes. Such devices were viewed as inconsistent with the openness and flexibility required by 1960s progressivism, and indeed in many schools planning in any form became anathema. Record-books listing intentions were replaced by retrospective diaries of events, and schemes fell into disuse, though rarely completely so in the case of mathematics and reading. The 1982 survey found most schools using 'guidelines' of some sort for language and mathematics, but the former tended to be restricted to reading, and perhaps writing, and to ignore spoken language, literature, poetry and drama. In other areas of the curriculum the situation was variable, and more than half the schools visited had no guidelines at all in areas other than mathematics, language, physical and religious education. Where schools had guidelines these were rarely exemplary in HMI's terms, but tended to contain merely lists of items to be taught and to offer little on ways of organising learning experiences. HMI viewed the connection between guidelines which were ill thought-out or absent altogether and curriculum superficiality, unevenness and inconsistency as a causal one.

The situation may not be that clear cut, not least because the absence, presence, on quality of curriculum guidelines can be viewed equally as a symptom rather than a cause of a school's outlook on a number of issues: the desirability of forward planning: the extent needed of such planning: the balance between individual class-teacher freedom and collective adherence to common procedures. It is this important to avoid naive overestimation of the impact of guidelines. They are only written words after all, a 'paper curriculum' rather than a curriculum in action, and the relative privacy enjoyed by primary teachers permits the possibility of a substantial gulf between words and deeds, even if the guidelines do not actively suffer the fate noted by teacher folklorists of 'gathering dust in the stock cupboard'.

This would suggest that if guidelines are to have any value they should be constructed on the basis of attention to strategies for their use as well as to their content. HMI seem to imply that quality of content is sufficient guarantee of success. I would suggest that the question of strategy be considered before the guidelines are written, not, as commonly happens, afterwards, since the characters of guidelines must obviously be consistent with their intended manner of use.

The central question is 'How can a written document influence class teacher practice?'. The usual answer is 'By being as comprehensive and a prescriptive as possible' and armed with this precept post-holder produce immaculate documents which may or may no have the impact they seek.

We are bound to consider the possibilities:

(a) that a scheme may be partly or even wholly unworkable for a particular teacher; (b) that, specialist expertise notwithstanding, a document may not be perfect; (c) that the more comprehensive it is, the more it may be seen to cast doubts upon the class teacher's competence.

Even if these are possibilities rather than actualities, they could suggest that the imposition of a 'definitive' scheme upon a group of teachers is an unwise strategy. In any even, apart from the practical, interpersonal and political objections, such an approach runs counter to the view of teacher autonomy postulated in this book which requires close intellectual engagement by the teacher in the activities relevant to his task, and to the notion of a dynamic and responsive curriculum. A curriculum can never be 'definitive': nor therefore can a curriculum document.

It would seem that it may be more sensible to consider an alternative strategy whereby no scheme produced by one individual has more than 'working paper' or 'draft' status, and the nearest a school comes to a definitive statement is a document which is the product of substantial collective discussion and is subjected to regular review and modification in the light of both the experience of implementing it and of changing circumstances. It is worth noting that HMI views on this matter in the latest of the succession of phase surveys, that on 9-13 middle schools, shifted towards a greater concern with strategy. They too now argued for 'working documents' rather than polished 'schemes'.

This is not to argue that the content of a curriculum scheme should be vague or meagre. On the contrary, provided its status is understood, the more detail it offers the higher the level of debate it can provoke. In this respect HMI are right to castigate those schemes which provide subject-matter checklists and give no attention to pedagogy.

Equally, however, we must be alive to the conceptual and ideological dimensions of curriculum documents: they embody views of the children and the education process. All such views are inherently challengeable.

We should recognise that this essentially means-ends view of learning is not the only one available and, at the very least, it must cause us to ask, along with the critics of behavioural objectives, whether it is either desirable or possible to specify learning objectives and strategies in advance in this way for all pupils and for all areas of the curriculum. I do not wish to dwell on the debate about behavioural objectives, 'expressive' objectives and 'principles of procedure': it is a field well covered in the curriculum literature. But it must be said that the writing of a scheme by a post-holder, and the discussion of a scheme by fellow-teachers ought to be undertaken with some sensitivity to these issues. Blenkin and Kelly rightly point out that such sensitivity is as yet in short supply in as far as one particular model of curriculum planning, the Tyler-Bloom objectives model, tactility inderpins many of the curriculum documents and packages of recent years. I have already identified this tendency in initial training courses: readers can discover for themselves the same tendency in the many curriculum policy documents emerging from LEAs in the wake of DES circular 6/81 as well as in school schemes.

Thus, if there is to be prescription as to what a curriculum document should include it should be self-conscious and open-ended: a rationale for a curriculum area, which may or may not include specific aims and objectives; a statement of the possible content or subject-matter to be encountered rather that, necessarily, a list of concepts to be 'covered'; indicators as to alternative teaching and learning strategies - which focus teachers' attention on the decisions to be taken in matters like children' groupings, the uses of individual, group and class work, the use of resources, but do not pre-empty those decisions; and suggestions as to criteria, means and purposes of evaluating children's learning which do not necessarily presuppose testing and allow for the appraisal of learning processes as well as outcomes.

A curriculum working paper, then, might best be conceived as incorporating what Stenhouse terms 'principles of procedure' whereby decisions may be taken and justified with respect to intentions, the selection of content, the development of a teaching strategy, the sequencing of learning, the diagnosis of individual children's needs, strengths and weaknesses.

Such an approach, I suggest, is some way from the definitive and authoritarian uses of guidelines implied in the two HMI primary surveys.

Staff meetings, whether in connection with curriculum documents or for other purposes are another current growth points. The relative intimacy of primary schools has sometimes served to justify heads' avoidance of formal staff meetings: HMI criticised the heavy reliance on 'informal gatherings at break or launch times'. But formal meetings may have been resisted by heads for other reasons, to do less with school size than the assumption that curriculum and policy matters where not open to debate and that residual matters - like arrangements for Christmas parties, sports days and playground supervision - could be dealt with either informally or by the issuing of directives and notes. HMI, however, clearly regarded formal meetings as an essential ingredient of curriculum planning, consistent with their view that teachers should play a greater part in the formulation of school policy.

As with schemes and guidelines the issues here are both practical and conceptual. Staff meetings can engender a sense of collective commitment; they can help teachers towards an understanding of and involvement in whole school concerns; open up the individual teacher to alternative arguments and ideas; stimulate intellectual engagement; minimise curriculum in coherence and inconsistency: in short, staff meetings are potentially one way of realising both the concept of a 'whole curriculum' as discussed in these pages and the notion of the autonomous teacher. Equally, staff meetings can consist of headteacher monologues, aimless and trivial anecdote-swapping or opinion-parading, frustrating to staff and head alike.

This kind of scenario prompts some to emphasise efficiency and instrumentality in respect of staff meetings: the need for a clearly defined and realistic agenda, circulated in advance; the need for input to meetings, to avoid off-the-top-of-the-head discussion, in the form of previously circulated discussion or working papers; the need for meetings to be firmly chaired so as to ensure progress through the agenda, to enable all staff to contribute and achieve a tangible outcome; the need for decisions to be ratified and minuted.

Such procedural aspects are undoubtedly important. At the same time, the act of formalising professional discourse politicises the process to an extent which those steeped in the relatively informal primary tradition may not apprehend. Procedures facilitate manipulation of the direction of discussion and decisions. They promote the stronger divergence of the two levels of discourse and meaning to some extent present in most human interaction - the spoken and the unspoken, the text and the subtext. They provide fertile ground for rhetoric and populism, for what Bailey in his anthropological study of committees, calls 'The tactical uses of passion'. The formal meeting adopts par excellence the trappings of rationality, but it feeds and legitimises irrationality, cynicism, insincerity and manipulation. It requires polite consensus. Yet it may deal with issues on which consensus is unachievable: in which case votes have to be taken and dissent to the tune of 49.9 per cent can remain as an unresolved embarrassment, a reminder not so much that the decision was 'right', or had 'majority support', as that the issue was of such complexity or controversy that to force a vote was the least appropriate way to deal with it: a vote 'for' or 'against' implies the existence of only two points of view.

Such consequences of bureaucratising human interaction are especially marked in large institutions where an added complexity is that the few individuals gathered together may represent or claim to represent many others, so that the committee or broad manifests the maneuvering or sectional interests, the problem of the real or claimed mandate from absent constituents, and the heightening of the power and game-playing dimensions of the whole process.

Committees in this charecterisation are an overwhelmingly male preserve. That being so, many women teachers may be instinctively less comfortable in such circumstances than men, who may actually revel in the ritualised aggression and sometimes bogus instrumentality. They may feel themselves disadvantaged by the style of the procedure to an extent which they would not in a less circumscribed situation, and therefore unable to make the kind of contribution of which they are capable.

There are further, conceptual, grounds for questioning this approach however: is it compatible with the nature of curriculum and curriculum issues as we have defined them in this book?

We have characterised curriculum issues as having several dimensions: cultural, epistemological, psychological, pedagogical, planning and evaluation, and value. It will perhaps be acknowledged by now that the last is the most fundamental and pervasive in that value-issue underpin all the others. This is a diagnosis shared by Reid who sees curriculum problems as predominantly *practical*, yet in a *moral* rather than a *technical* sense, so that few of them yield ready certainties. He criticises mainstream curriculum theory for its pursuit of rationalism at the expense of proper exploration of the moral dimension, and bureaucratic decision-making for forcing curriculum debate into a mould where 'procedure, majority votes and authoritative pronouncements have... usurped the place of appreciation, deliberation and judgment'. Each of these latter three words is used carefully: *appreciation* of a problem demands analysis of its many facets and possibly a variety of 'expert' perspectives to elucidate these; *judgement* invokes both a practical capacity and a sense of and discrimination among differing values; *deliberation* is used in preference to 'debate' because the latter presumes the existence of final and correct answers. One might add that 'debate' also suggests a contest between a maximum of two viewpoints, one usually the antithesis of the other. Deliberation, in contrast, is a multi-faceted collective process of seeking to understand complexity; its practical essence is informality and the absence of threat so that members will be prepared both to risk and context assertions. Deliberation, I would suggest, is the collective pursuit of that 'theorising' which I argued should come to replace 'recipe theory' in both initial teacher training and everyday teacher discourse.

Reid's notion of 'deliberation' is consistent with the approach to curriculum this book has taken, to an extent that bureaucratised discourse is not. On the other hand 'deliberation' is vastly more disciplined and informed than that which highly formalised staff meetings seek to replace, namely random, anecdotal chat. There has to be a middle ground between inhibiting structure and debilitating flaccidity.

Equally pertinent is Reid's suggestion that the optimum group number for deliberation is ten or twelve people in that it enables different sources of expertise to be represented without the tendency to excessive formality associated with larger groups. A medium-sized primary school has that number of staff, and it could be argued in any case that the size and cultural tradition of primary schools makes them less vulnerable to the bureaucratic excesses of, for example, higher education institutions.

Difficulties arise, however, in relation to the view that deliberation requires a range of expertise. For as long as primary teachers define themselves as experts only on primary children this diversity may be unavailable. But the gradual legitimation of specialists, in the wake of the 1978 HMI survey, may make for conditions in which the specialist contribution to policy is accepted and indeed forestered, provided—as we saw earlier - that the threat potential to head and class teacher can be neutralised.

Perhaps, therefore, in the allocation of responsibility posts schools should attend to four further than two types of responsibility. First, the curriculum areas, second, a particular age-range of children, third, one of the central dimensions of curriculum analysis and planning, and fourth, various school odd jobs. Thus through selective study and experience an individual teacher might claim general proficiency as a class teacher together with specialist expertise in, for example, environmental studies, the education of 7-9-year-olds, and curriculum evaluation; or in mathematics, the education of 9-11-year-olds, and pedagogy/classroom organisation. The 'odd jobs' can surely be fairly distributed on the basis of choice or rotation: 'notice broads' hardly requires a course o advanced study.

This line of speculation is one which schools might profitably pursue: in any case it could be argued that, regardless of the meetings/ deliberation issue, the concept of 'specialist' adduced by HMI should not be accepted at face value since it is very narrowly premised. The nature of primary teaching requires professional specialisation in areas additional to the conventional subjects:

> To conceive to 'curriculum' as HMI appear to, in conventional subject terms, will tend to produce a notion of specialism which excludes *cross-curricular* concerns. A more comprehensive concept of specialisation—'professional" rather than merely 'subject'—is ... to be preferred.

Evaluation: beyond checklists

A further strategy to achieve prominence in recent years is formal evaluation. Two uses or justifications are generally cited: public accountability and staff/school development. Thus on the one hand we have increasingly elaborate documentary procedures for providing information about pupils, teachers and curriculum to heads, LEAs, parents and other schools: and, on the other, procedures for generating individual or collective review of teaching, curriculum and policy as a basis for change and development. One responds to external demand, the other to what are seen as fundamental professional imperatives; one provides information for consumption outside the school, the other is an internal matter.

Despite these essentially different purposes and requirements the two activities are frequently treated as necessitating identical or similar procedures. The commonest such procedure is the checklist, which in recent years has become such an ubiquitous feature of the educational scene that many find it hard to accept that it is neither necessarily the only nor the best way of meeting accountability requirements, let alone of promoting professional development. Checklists are now constructed by LEAs and schools as a basis for three sorts of evaluation: pupils, of teachers and of schools. Their essence is a set of questions or items requiring answers or scores; sometimes, as in the case of pupil records, in the form of ticks or literal/numerical grades-scores; elsewhere, as with some of the school self-evaluation checklists, they are more agenda for discussion.

Thus, while most LEAs have recorded cards. Rochdale LEA has a book for each pupil which has to be completed for each school year in respect of detailed lists of concepts, skills and qualities. Inner London LEA, one of the pioneers of school self-evaluation, has its now widely used document 'Keeping the school under review' which offers an extended list of questions about children, parental involvement, curriculum, organisation, staffing and staff roles 'to assist a school to examine its organisation, its resources, its standards of achievement and its relationships'. Another pioneering LEA, Salford, shifted from an overt accountability approach, with a detailed primary school self-evaluation booklet requesting the transmission to 'the office' of regular detailed information on facets of schools life from the state of the buildings to curriculum areas, resources, community relations and management, to a version which combined accounting to the LEA with school self-assessment 'as a contribution to staff development ... and ... curricular and organizational developments'.

Detailed analysis of the contents and procedural implications of such documents is now available elsewhere; the most extensive are by Elliott, and by Clift, Weiner and Wilson. Much of the discussion is concerned with technical aspects - format, categories of questions, intended mode of use, problems of clarity, ambiguity, time required for completing checklists and record cards/books, and so on. Because checklists and elaborated record-keeping systems are now a fact of school life it is inevitable that such factors should weight heavily, for above all these procedures are time-consuming.

Becher, Eraut and Knight, dealing specifically with these practices as used in primary schools, are among the commentators who draw attention to some rather more fundamental problems of this approach. One is the checklist or record card's implicit view of whatever is being reviewed - children's language, teacher's use of resources, schools' relationships with parents, for example. By asking, or giving priority to, some questions rather than others, the head or LEA responsible implies a preferred model. Thus, as we saw, LEAs like Avon expect teachers to rate children's writing in terms of the Bullock Report's categories of 'transactional', 'expressive' and 'poetic' and to appraise children's use of language (oral) in terms of Joan Tough's categories of 'elf-maintaining', 'directing', 'reporting', 'reasoning', 'predicting', 'projecting' and so on. Apart from the fact that these are indeed only models of language, it appears to be tacitly assumed that teachers completing the cards have the requisite understanding of what such categories mean.

In this regard the danger in such approaches is their apparent but often spurious objectivity. Putting a tick or a number against a word like 'predicting' may seem to some teachers to be more objective than writing an opinion in an empty box. In fact, both activities are heavily value-laden, the letter in an obvious way, the former more profoundly so because the vagaries of personal opinion are compounded by another person's values and by problems of interpretation, meaning and judgement.

In contrast some such devices are so obviously tendentious as to be ludicrous and therefore, paradoxically, less dangerous in use. An example is the checklist sent to me in place of the more usual invitation to write a reference on a teacher. This required ratings on a five-point scale on such items as: 'skill in putting into practice good principles of teaching, judged largely by results; energetic, even-tempered; pleasing, attractive, appropriately dressed, wholesome influence; success in making social contacts; aggressiveness and initiates; intellectual alertness - native mental endowment as distinguished from acquired abilities; freedom from social indiscretions...'. No further comment is needed.

The second problem is the lack of attention in

some such documents to strategy. As Becher, Eraut and Knight remark.

To the outside world, checklists to offer an interesting compromise between external guidance and authority and internal choice and responsibility. But within the school itself their strong management-orientation can seem to belie their declared purpose of guiding self-evaluation.

This dilemma is not necessarily resolved by stressing the development function while elaborating the preferred strategy., The strength of the Schools Council/Bristol University 'GRIDS' approach is that it provides detailed guidance on school self-review strategy as a cyclic process and specifies the various steps and tasks to be undertaken. This contrasts with the more familiar LEA approach of merely sending the school a list of questions to be answered. The GRIDS booklet also emphasises the importance of grounding strategy in key principles or commitments in areas like consultation and staff involvement. In this respect it is comparable to this author's development of an evaluation 'constitution' for a Manchester college', though the latter was considerably more detailed and covered issues like confidentiality, dissemination and the vital matter of who controls the various decisions which an evaluation requires. Where GRIDS fails to escape the dilemma is its tacit vesting of such control with the head, so that although there is consultation about topics for review and the implications of view for development these are firmly circumscribed by the head's decision over who should be involved and in precisely what capacity.

Formalised self-evaluation them, is not simply a matter of asking and answering questions, completing forms and cards: it requires elucidation of more fundamental matters concerning schools' and teachers' value-systems in respect of children, curriculum and teaching on the one hand, and school decision-making, and professional relationships and responsibilities on the other.

The external accountability functions of evaluation procedures can be reduced in favour of 'development', but the internal accountability dimension remains pervasive. Formalised evaluation is pre-eminently a management tool and underpinning every style of management is a view of the accountability relations and obligations of the institution whose members and affairs are begin managed.

Thus we could, and should, extend our list of the dimensions of formalised evaluation, by analysing the kinds of decisions which all such evaluation necessarily entails.

Formal evaluation: the main decisions

1. Decisions about the *aims* of evaluation. What is it for.
2. Decisions about the *focus* of evaluation. What aspects of school life are to be evaluated.
3. Decisions about the *criteria* for evaluation. What will be the nature of the criteria for

judging the worth and/or effectiveness of the aspects of school life to be studied?

4. Decisions about the *methods* of evaluation to be used. Evaluation is a judgement based on evidence. What will be the character and source of the evidence?

5. Decisions about *organisation.* How will the evaluation be conducted.

6. Decisions about *dissemination.* What means for recording and reporting evaluation judgements will be used? To whom will they be available? To whom will they be available? What will be the extent of confidentiality?

7. Decisions about *application.* To what uses will evaluations be put, and how will they enabled to inform decision-making.

8. Decisions about *control* and *accountability.* This is the overriding decision because is determines the direction of the answers to all the other questions. Who, then, decides? Head, individual teachers, teachers collectively, or LEA advisors?

These questions provide the kind of framework needed if formalised evaluation is to establish some degree of methodological, educational and institutional legitimacy. They also imply a further prerequisite, that of subjecting the whole matter of evaluation strategy to discussion with the school. Evaluation is about values and valuing; for the head to ask and answer the above questions without reference to colleagues is to imply the paramountcy or superiority of his values. Yet most of the questions by their nature can only properly be approached through open discussion. Other evaluation decisions demand diverse sorts of expertise - in curriculum areas, in children's development and learning, in evaluation techniques - which in respect of the scope of primary education no one teacher or head can posses. Evaluation is pre-eminently an issue for which the 'deliberation' we discussed in the previous section is a necessity. Viewed in this more comprehensive manner, the managerialist/ technicist approach through improved checklists gives added cause for anxiety.

Formal and informal evaluation: barking up the wrong tree?

The development of procedures for formal evaluation, we have seen, may all to frequently neglect the central issues discussed above, but even more fundamentally, it may tend to imply two questionable assumptions: first, that such procedures constitute the most valid forms of evaluation; second, that their arrival heralds the end of an earlier era of non-evaluation.

Throughout the discussion on this topic I have used the adjective 'formal' or 'formalised' in order to emphasise both the official and artificial character of such evaluation procedures, and to allow for a contrast with other sorts of evaluation which can reasonably be termed 'informal'. We can define evaluation in the curriculum theorist's terms as 'information for decision-makers' or as 'measurement of the extent to which objectives are achieved' (both of them problematic and prescriptive rather than neutral and descriptive); or we can seek a more open definition like 'making judgements of worth or effectiveness'. Note, as against this, how limited are the first two definitions in terms of our eight evaluation decisions listed above: one views evaluation mainly in terms of decisions and the other terms of decision. Both neglect the vital areas of values, criteria, control and accountability.

If we adopt the third definition, it allows for three extensions to our conceptual framework. One is to project to centre-stage the actual *judgemental process* at the heart of evaluation; the second is to free it from presuppositions about particular methodologies, contexts or uses; the third is to prompt a sense of evaluation as a continuum of many diverse types and modes of judgement, all of which can make a claim to be taken seriously, not because they are 'formal' rather than 'private' or 'informal' but because they happen, they occur in real life.

This judgemental continuum, in schools and classrooms, overwhelmingly comprises evaluations which are nearer its 'informal' than its 'formal' pole. Teachers and heads use of tests, checklists, profiles and so on constitutes a minute proportion of the evaluation on which their most important everyday decisions are made. The *focus* is children's personalities, their potential, their behaviour, their educational progress. The *aims* are diagnosis, making necessarily rapid decisions as a basis for further action. The *criteria* are personal, experimental, value-loaded, sometimes idiosyncratic, sometimes collectives evolved. The *methods* are watching, talking, listening, giving out and receiving non-verbal cues and signals, reflecting, hypothesising, discussing...

Evaluation in this sense is of fundamental importance in schools and classrooms because it is basic to human behaviour and interaction. It is a process of immense subtlety and, for the child or teacher being evaluated, of profound consequence. And it works no less effectively than tests and checklists in providing a reliable basis for diagnosis and action. Indeed, HMI argue in the 9-13 survey that such formal procedures tend to neglect this latter, diagnostic, dimension and concentrate overmuch on generalised and summative judgements of attainment.

Nor is it the case as we have seen that 'formal' procedures necessarily have a stronger claim to 'objectivity' than informal: formal procedures are more accessible to public scrutiny than informal and thus can more readily be checked for bias, but this does not of itself guarantee their objectivity.

The realistic approach in this matter would seem to be not to replace everyday informal evaluation but to refine it. It may or may not be always valid or reliable, but its ubiquity and dominance demand our attention.

School self-evaluation, then, would seem to require first that teachers and heads develop a proper self-consciousness about their everyday appraisals and judgements, then that they device ways of refining them further, supplementing them where appropriate by more formalised procedures. The questions for schools are less 'How *shall* we evaluate?' than 'How *do* we evaluate?' and 'How valid and effective is our evaluation?' The focus of such appraisal then becomes the schools central evaluations: the everybody, minute-to-minute ways in which teachers assess children's progress, define their needs, judge their potential, and decide what curriculum experiences to provide; the ways heads determine curriculum policies and priorities, and assess staff competence and progress. The dimensions of this appraisal can be those same decisions of which 'formal' evaluation is constituted—aims, focus, content, criteria, methods and so on.

The processes under scrutiny, in effect, are those we have examined in this book, though the word 'evaluation' was not necessarily used: the teacher's judgements about the nature and purposes of primary education, about childhood and individual children, about teaching strategies, about appropriate curriculum experiences; teachers' and heads' judgements about the whole curriculum, school staff' individual or collective judgement about school policy and decision-making. A large part of this book is essentially an examination of evaluations and evaluation capacities in primary education.

All this implies an important shift in consciousness. The evaluation movement has seemed to imply that hitherto teachers did not evaluate, or at least did so inadequately. The parallel with initial teacher education is not coincidental: there the assumption, we saw, was that teachers operate without theory, without a valid view of children, curriculum teaching and learning. In teacher education a recipe theory has been imposed on students and teachers without regard to existing everyday theories and theorising process. In evaluation a predetermined set of focuses, criteria and methods is imposed without regard for existing evaluative processes. Both tendencies are a consequence of factors we have touched on at various points in the book: the failure of the primary teaching profession to develop an adequately rational and generalisable language of discourse about its tasks and activities which could hold its own against that of academics, researchers and policy-makers; the acquiescence of the profession in the elevation of the one sort of language and the one sort of activity over their own; their acceptance of an over-simplified and scientistic view of knowledge which unduly favoured the claims to 'fact' and 'proof' of social scientists and evaluation technists; the power differential in such matters between the class teacher on the one hand, and the academic researcher, LEA adviser to administrator on the other; the presumptuousness of some in the latter groups concerning the relative merits of their own and teachers' procedures; the exacerbation of these tendencies (a) by a dominant primary school culture which isolates and parochialises the class teacher and (b) by teachers' lack of influence, relative to other groups in the educational world, on the vehicles for generating and disseminating ideas—books, journals, conferences and professional networks.

The debate about school self-evaluation, like that about educational theory, has become skewed away from the teacher from classroom and from classroom actualities, not least because of teachers' failure to participate in it.

Index